Seek My Face

The scriptural basis of 'seeking the Lord'.

DAVID M. ADAMS

**Kingdom Faith Church,
Leicester UK 1999**

RPP
ROPERPENBERTHY PUBLISHING

Unless other wise stated, scripture is taken from the
HOLY BIBLE, NEW INTERNATIONAL VERSION.
Copyright © 1973, 1978, 1984,
by International Bible Society
Used by permission of
Hodder & Stoughton Ltd.

Published by RoperPenberthy Publishing Ltd
PO Box 545, Horsham, RH12 4QW

Text copyright © David M. Adams 2001

The moral right of the author has been asserted in accordance with the
Copyright Designs and Patent Act 1988

First Published 2001

ISBN 1 903905 08 7

All rights reserved. No part of this publication may be reproduced in any material
form (including photocopying or storing it in any medium by electronic means)
without the prior written permission of the publisher or under licence from the
Copyright Licensing Agency, 90 Tottenham Court Road, London WC1 9HE.

Printed in the United Kingdom.

DEDICATION

This book is dedicated to the members of Kingdom Faith Church, Leicester, and to those who have worshipped and sought God with us.
Most of what I have learned about the things written in this book has been in the context of leading them. Without their wholehearted devotion to worshipping God and seeking his face, this book would not have been possible.

Other books by David M. Adams.

The Bare Necessities of Faith.

Spiritual Authority

CONTENTS

INTRODUCTION

1	**Intimacy with God.**	**17**
	Paradise lost.	17
	Love is the key.	18
	God's plan for restoration	19
	The wife of Jehovah and the bride of Christ.	19
	The new covenant.	20
	Seek my face.	20
2	**Seeking the Lord.**	**22**
	Man's approach to God.	22
	From OT to NT.	23
	Priests and the tabernacle.	25
	A mediator is needed.	26
	Jesus' ministry prefigured.	29
	A new law.	32
	Jesus our High Priest.	33
3	**Meeting with God.**	**36**
	Seeking the Lord.	36
	The words.	37
	With all my heart.	37
	You will find me.	39
	You will meet with me.	40
4	**Why Seek God?**	**44**
	It's what he wants and commands.	44
	To allow him to search our hearts.	45
	To build a personal relationship with him.	46
	To seek his counsel, wisdom and guidance.	47
	Benefits of seeking God.	50

	The life and joy of the Lord are ours.	50
	We are strengthened and blessed.	51
	We, the church, and the nation are prospered.	51
	Consequences of not seeking the Lord.	53
	Marriage is the model.	54

5   Behold Your God.   56

By faith.	56
God's character.	56
Relationship is the key.	58
I the Lord am holy.	58
The word *qodesh*.	58
The word *cherem*.	59
The word *chol*.	60
Holiness does not mean remoteness.	60
What is holy?	61
God's holy people.	62
Our part.	62

6   God is Love.   64

Love: the words *ahaba* & *agape*.	64
Mercy: the word *chesed*.	65
Compassion: the word *râcham*.	66
Grace.	67
Patience.	69
Faithfulness.	69
Résumé.	71

7   Jesus our High Priest.   72

Christianity is Jewish.	72
Hebrews 9:4.	75
Jesus our High Priest.	76

	Jesus represents God to us.	77
	Jesus strengthens us for battle.	77
	Jesus intercedes for us.	78
	Jesus is our brother.	80

8   Ministry to God.   84

Royal priesthood.	84
Ministry to God.	85
Worship.	86
The first court.	87
Silence in worship.	88
The second and third courts.	89
Leading worship.	90
Two distinct functions.	91
Preparing to lead worship.	91
Spirit-led worship.	92
The music group.	92
Dear Pastor.	93
Worship and sacrifice.	94
You have an open heaven.	95

9   How to seek the Lord.   97

Seeking the Lord takes time.	97
Then I understood.	99
Righteousness and seeking God.	101
Who am I?	

10   In practice.   105

Relationships are the key indicator.	105
Practical matters.	106
Start by allaying fears.	107
Get into thanksgiving, praise and worship.	107

Be real.	108
Healing of memories.	110
Direct counselling.	111
Meeting with God.	112
How do you know?	113
The voice of God.	114

11 Living in the glory. 119

The Jerusalem temple.	117
With God in the Most Holy Place.	118
Solomon's throne.	118
Queen Esther: Intimacy with God.	119
The lifestyle of the Most Holy Place.	120
God's rest.	120
Ministry to man.	123

REFERENCES

SCRIPTURE INDEX

PREFACE

I had no intention of writing this little book. It began as a collection of scriptures and notes, a handout, for use in one of our 'seeking the Lord' days, but God didn't leave it there. Throughout the next year I was led to study and meditate upon the scriptural basis of seeking God. In this process he has drawn me closer to himself, and he will do the same for you as you follow the Spirit along the same track.

It was as a student at Kingdom Faith Bible College, Horsham, that I first came under this teaching through the ministry of Colin Urquhart. I shall never forget that first occasion on which he told us that the scriptures show how to meet with God, and then led us to do just that. It changed my life and my ministry. Since then I have been privileged to lead many people in the same way, and have seen their lives dramatically changed too.

I believe that this teaching is urgently needed by the church in our day, and that that is why I have been led to write down what I have learned and experienced. As Christ's return draws near, the Father is lifting the heads and eyes of his true church to see Jesus, and to focus upon him as never before. To him be the glory, for evermore.

David M. Adams
Kingdom Faith Church
Leicester UK
Easter 1999

INTRODUCTION

Truly you are a God who hides himself. (Isaiah 45:15)

God created mankind to know him and to enjoy intimate fellowship with him. Hence the oft-repeated biblical commands to *seek my face* and to *seek the Lord*. Scripture clearly differentiates 'seeking the Lord' from the associated activities of praise, prayer and worship. These activities overlap and are closely related but each has a distinctive content. Together with the allied concepts of 'watching', 'waiting' and 'enquiring', these scriptures leave no doubt that God's heart is for a people who will commit themselves to forming and maintaining with him an intimate relationship of love and trust, and that he mightily blesses those who do so.

To travel this path is to go beyond that basic knowledge of the gospel needed for conversion and which is inadequate to take the believer on to maturity. Many remain babes in Christ through ignorance, laziness, or lack of leadership. Only those who stir up the gift of God within them, who press on to perfection, inherit in practice and reality the full blessings of the new covenant won for us by Christ.

The aim of this little book is to give a simple outline of biblical teaching on this issue, and to indicate how it may work in practice, especially in corporate situations. To seek God is to submit to his Spirit according to his written word, the Bible. Therefore, as in any Spirit-led activity, there can be no set formula. My own experience, especially when leading groups or churches in this activity, is that it is never the same twice over. Nevertheless, what we do need to know and understand is the scriptural basis of seeking God's face. That is what I have attempted to supply here. I have also included some comments based upon my own experience of leading others in seeking God.

CHAPTER 1

Intimacy With God

In the beginning.
 Before the world, or anything else, was created, there was God: Father, Son and Holy Spirit relating in such perfection of love and intimacy that they could describe themselves only as One. True love and intimacy long to be shared. Therefore God said: *"Let us make man in our image, in our likeness" (Genesis 1:26).*

Let us put in him a desire for love, intimacy and beauty. Let us pour out our love upon him, and enjoy his love and devotion in return. Let there be a transparent trust and intimacy between us and him. Let us prepare things for him to do and achieve that will rejoice his heart. And because love is true only if it is given from the heart, let us give him freedom of choice. Let us create a place for him to be, let him rule over it, name the plants and animals, and make things so that we may take joy in his creative initiatives. Therefore, the Lord God planted a garden *"in Eden, and there he put the man he had formed" (Genesis 2:8).*

But God who made the stars is not starry-eyed. The Trinity knew all too well where the gift of freewill, essential to true love, would lead. Father, Son and Spirit, seeing into each other's hearts knew that, nevertheless, they would never stop pursuing and loving man regardless of cost, and that in the end some would chose to return their love freely and wholeheartedly.

Paradise lost.

The Bible opens with a glimpse of man living in Eden in unrestricted fellowship with his Creator, enjoying face-to-face communion. Adam and Eve lost that through disobedience. Being ejected from Eden in consequence, man's relationship with God was thenceforth possible only at a distance. Nevertheless, at once, God's merciful heart was shown in covering their nakedness. This act conveyed both his refusal to let the relationship lapse, and a hint of the cost of restoration in that an animal died to provide the skin from which their clothes were made.

This simple account fails to do justice to the awesome spiritual consequences of Adam and Eve's sin. "When Adam fell ... God removed the seat of his presence with man from earth to heaven" (F. Bartelman)[1]. Thus, as the apostle Paul would write millennia later, Adam and Eve were left *without hope and without God in the world (Ephesians 2:12).*

Fear shot through their limbs and gripped their hearts as in shock they realised their nakedness. Then, cringing before God, the consequences rained down like hammer blows on an anvil: a change in their own relationship, pain in childbirth, hard labour in the fields. Finally, the crowning agony, banished from the garden and from God's presence for ever. Jesus' anguished cry from the cross as the burden of the world's sin separated him from the Father's presence was theirs first.

The Bible is the story of God whose nature is love and who, in spite of the repeated disobedience, indifference and failure of those to whom he has given everything, refuses to give up on them. He is love. He is full of mercy, compassion and grace, and free of condemnation. And because he always does what he says he will do, he will bring at least a remnant of his creation into that relationship of unconditional mutual love which has been his intent from before the foundation of the world. That determination is proved by the story that unfolded from Adam and Eve onwards, and is still not finished.

> "God has paid us the intolerable compliment of loving us in the deepest, most tragic, most inexorable sense." (C.S. Lewis)

> "The Bible is the story of a romance, a heavenly Father seeking an earthly bride for his Son." (David Pawson)

Love is the key.
The Bible both opens and closes with scenes in which God and man are in unclouded, intimate fellowship. Adam and Eve lost their intimacy with God through disobedience and sin but the final scenes of the Bible show that the church, now revealed as the new Jerusalem, finally enjoys an even more profound fellowship with God than did Adam and Eve.

> *I saw the Holy City, the new Jerusalem, coming down out of heaven from God, prepared as a bride beautifully dressed for her husband. And I heard a loud voice from the throne saying, "Now the dwelling of God is with men, and he will live with them. They will be his people, and God himself will be with them and be their God"* (Revelation 21:2-3).

Our concern now is with what happens between these opening and closing scenes of the Bible. It is, of course, a complex story and for that reason alone it is easy to lose sight of the purpose of it, which is to restore intimate fellowship between God and man. God created mankind to know him, to be loved by him, and to respond to him in love and obedience. The grand theme of the Bible is about how God is restoring us to this condition. This alone should give us a fresh understanding of the value he places on each person.

God's plan for restoration.

Despite the separation now established between man and his Creator, God nevertheless continued to speak to his people with words of promise, comfort and encouragement. Many centuries before God's revelations to Moses, Jacob was even granted a preview of a pathway between heaven and earth.

In the millennia after Adam and Eve God gradually revealed his scheme for restoration of Eden-like life and communion with man, a scheme in three stages. First, a long preparatory phase (the OT and inter-testamental period), leading to a brief transitional stage (incarnation to Pentecost); then, finally, the Church age, at least two further millennia, concluding with the return of Christ to earth, and renewal of Eden-like communion.

The wife of Jehovah and the bride of Christ.

Since God's whole purpose in creating man is to relate to him in love and trust, he speaks repeatedly about relationships. Because marriage is the most exclusive and intimate of human relationships, God speaks in those terms so that we shall see that he looks for a like response from us. Thus from the announcement that *"I will be your God and you will be my people" (Exodus 6:7; Jeremiah 7:23, 11:4; Ezekiel 36:28)* the revelation progresses to the statement that God views Israel as his wife *(Deuteronomy 6:10-15;7:6-11;Ezekiel 16:8)* and looks for an appropriate response.

Intimacy is at the heart of God's being and nature. Made in his image, we too crave intimacy. If we do not find it in him who alone can meet that need, we try all manner of substitutes, but none of them satisfies absolutely the deepest need of our heart, not even the best of marriages.

Israel's unfaithfulness to her 'husband' led to separation *(Isaiah 50:1)* and then divorce *(Jeremiah 3:6-10)*. However, God who is rich in mercy did not leave Israel bereft but spoke through the prophets of a new covenant on which basis remarriage would occur. The difference between the new covenant and the old one is almost like that between an arranged marriage and a love match.

The new covenant.
In the NT this theme of God's desire for an intimate relationship with man is both confirmed and greatly extended. Jesus reaffirmed the greatest commandment: *"Love the Lord your God with all your heart and with all your soul and with all your mind and with all your strength" (Mark 12:30).* Then, by his death, resurrection and exaltation, he opened the way for an entirely new level of intimacy between God and man, of which the tearing of the temple curtain is symbolic. The NT believer has received the prophesied blessings of a new spirit and a new heart inscribed with God's law *(Ezekiel 36:26; Jeremiah 31:33).*

Now, because of Jesus, the believer is seen as part of Christ's body, having a righteousness that is by faith in him, indwelt by his Spirit, and admitted thereby to the ultimate in spiritual intimacy on earth, actually partaking of the divine nature *(2 Peter 1:4).* Nevertheless, this is still only a 'deposit', a foretaste of what is to come. The church is not yet the bride of Christ but she is betrothed to him, and is in the process of making herself ready for marriage. Before this happens, Christ will return to earth, there to reign with the saints. Thus, the seat of God's presence will be restored to earth for a millennium, reversing what happened in Eden.

When God's restoration plan is fully completed, his people will stand before his throne in their spiritual bodies, able now to see his face and to bear the full glory of his presence. Relieved by the gift of eternal life lived in spiritual bodies from the need to reproduce, with its attendant distractions, the Father will enjoy the undivided adoration of that remnant of his now sexless creation who have chosen to bow the knee to him and not to Satan.

Seek my face.
It is within the context of this grand design that God calls his people in every age to seek his face, to enjoy unclouded and intimate fellowship with him. Although it may seem to man that he is doing the seeking, in truth it is God who does the seeking and the drawing in love. We are simply responding to the unceasing grace and love of the One who never gives up on us. The reality is that God's reason for creation is love.

God has given every believer the astonishing intimacy of the indwelling Holy Spirit. Many can witness to the glorious fellowship with God that became theirs when they were filled with the Holy Spirit. Nevertheless, the demands of daily life require us to redirect our attention for much of the time, although it is possible to practice dwelling in the presence of God in all circumstances. Sadly, our common experience is that it is all too easy to lose our first love and to drift from the intimacy with God that once we enjoyed. Hence, the oft-repeated calls in scripture to 'seek my face', and therefore to give quality time to that most important of all relationships. Every lover and parent knows the deep longing to be given the undivided attention of the ones you love most, and how that longing builds up when circumstances delay it. Therefore, God says 'Seek my face'.

How blessed is God! And what a blessing he is! He's the Father of our Master, Jesus Christ, and takes us to the high places of blessing in him. Long before he laid down the earth's foundations, he had us in mind, had settled on us as the focus of his love, to be made whole and holy by his love. (Ephesians 1:3-4 The Message)

There is, then, a process of turning to God and of entering his presence. Whether, like the prodigal son we are returning to him from afar, or simply opening our hearts to him at the start of the day, there is a 'way' to be followed. This 'way' was the first thing revealed to Moses at Sinai, thereby indicating the importance God attaches to the manner in which his people approach him.

Chapter 2

Seeking The Lord

Man's approach to God.
The first major revelation of how God is to be approached was given to Moses on Mt. Sinai in the form of instructions for building a tabernacle *(Exodus 25-31)*. The word 'tabernacle' means 'the dwelling place of God's glory' *(cf. Psalm 26:8)*. It consisted of a luxurious tent set within an open-air courtyard. The tent had two compartments: an outer one, the Holy Place, and an inner one called the Holy of Holies or Most Holy Place, Figures 1 & 2. These three areas alone tell us of the possibility of a progress towards the heart of God of increasing intimacy.

Many books have been written on the complex and highly revealing symbolism of the tabernacle: here we note only the barest outline. Just within the outer courtyard was the bronze altar used for animal sacrifice. Beyond that stood a bronze washing bowl, made of mirrors. This, and the entire tent, was accessible only to the priests.

In the Holy Place stood three items of furniture. A seven-branched lamp stand (the menorah) fed with oil from a reservoir at the top was the only source of illumination, the flow of oil and the light representing the Holy Spirit. A golden table stood opposite it bearing consecrated bread: the priests replaced the bread each week, standing around the table to eat the older loaves, symbolic of fellowship around the word of God. Thirdly, a small golden altar stood near the curtain which divided the outer from the inner compartments: the priests would burn incense there, using censers with coals taken from the bronze altar, symbolising what would be the Spirit-led prayers and worship of believers, made possible by the sacrifice of Christ.

The inner compartment, the Most Holy Place, contained a single object: a chest, the ark of God, with two golden cherubim set over it on the lid. The light in this part of the tent was that of the presence and glory of God. Here, God told Moses, he would meet with him. Only the High Priest was allowed entry to this area, and then only once a year to make atonement for the nation by means of an offering of blood from a ritual sacrifice.

From OT to NT.

With the NT the picture is transformed dramatically. No tabernacle or temple is needed, for the Spirit of Jesus now dwells in the physical bodies of his servants who thereby become his temple and his body on earth. Thus, in OT days God had a temple for his people, but since Pentecost he has had a people for his temple.

A transition from OT symbolism to that of the NT is afforded by the divine physical act in which the veil of the Jerusalem temple was rent from top to bottom (and not the other way up, which could have been the work of vandals) at the moment of Jesus' death, showing that nothing now stands in the way of the most intimate communion of God with man.

The writer of *Hebrews* develops the symbolism in an astonishing insight, associating the tearing of Christ's body with that of the veil itself *(Hebrews 10:20)*. Indeed, the entire tabernacle symbolism collapses into a singularity as Christ is revealed as the

One in whom it all finds ultimate meaning and fulfilment, for he alone is the way to the Father. In the flow of blood and water *(John 19:34)* from God's wounded heart of love is seen the cleansing from sin foreshadowed by the activities at Moses' bronze altar and bowl, expressed so precisely by Augustus Toplady:

> Rock of Ages, cleft for me
> Let me hide myself in Thee
> Let the water and the blood
> From Thy riven side which flowed
> Be of sin the double cure
> Cleanse me from its guilt and power.

Jesus encouraged his followers to identify in him the fulfilment of the tabernacle symbolism. Declarations that he is *"the light of the world" (John 8:12)* and *"the bread of life" (John 6:35)* invite reference to the menorah and the table of the showbread, whilst his teaching on prayer with its comprehensive promises is consonant with the priestly work at the golden altar of incense. His dramatic claims of heavenly origin *(John 7:29, 8:23)*, and of being the exact representation of the Father *(John 14:9-11)* qualify for comparison with the function of the ark of the covenant. However, the claim that may well have had the greatest immediate impact upon his disciples was probably that he is *"the way, the truth, and the life" (John 14:6)*. Rabbinical tradition had labelled the entrances to the first, second and third courts of the tabernacle respectively as 'the way', 'the truth' and 'the life'.

> *In him [Jesus] and through faith in him we may approach God with freedom and confidence. (Ephesians 3:12)*
>
> *Therefore, brothers, since we have confidence to enter the Most Holy Place by the blood of Jesus, by a new and living way opened for us through the curtain, that is, his body, and since we have a great priest over the house of God, let us draw near to God with a sincere heart in full assurance of faith, having our hearts sprinkled to cleanse us from a guilty conscience and having our bodies washed with pure water. (Hebrews 10:19-22)*

Priests and the tabernacle.

The tabernacle of Moses was a visual aid, a model or paradigm of the way in which God is to be approached. It finds its meaning and fulfilment in Jesus who alone is the way to the Father. However, the tabernacle was not a museum piece: it was the place where the priests ministered to God. It was the focus of the life of the emergent nation of Israel, physically in that the tribes camped with it in their midst, Figure 1, and spiritually since it was there God spoke to Moses.

The tabernacle, with its associated rituals, had its limitations. Although provision was made for atonement for sins through the offering of sacrifices, the sins dealt with thereby were only inadvertent sins. No such provision was made for the more serious sins of the heart. Moreover, the priests themselves were denied entry to the Most Holy Place, except for an annual visit by the High Priest under conditions of the utmost solemnity. Jesus, in contrast, entered not a representation, which was in fact prohibited to him, but heaven itself in one final and all-sufficient act of atonement. This scene is transformed in the NT.

> *Therefore, my brothers, I want you to know that through Jesus the forgiveness of sins is proclaimed to you. Through him everyone who believes is justified from everything you could not be justified from by the law of Moses.*
> *(Acts 13:38-39)*

In the OT the priests were from the tribe of Levi, a tribe which God had chosen from out of the twelve tribes of Israel. Peter, writing to the church said:

> *But you are a chosen people, a royal priesthood, a holy nation, a people belonging to God, that you may declare the praises of him who called you out of darkness into his wonderful light. (1 Peter 2:9)*

This is the function of all who belong to Christ. Like the Levites, we have been chosen for this priestly role. We are a royal priesthood since we worship and minister to the King of kings. We

Seeking The Lord

are a *holy nation* since all who are Christ's are part of that kingdom of priests the Father desires. But in stark contrast to the Levitical priests, we are all granted entry to the Most Holy Place, and at all times. One thing has not changed: there is still only one High Priest.

A mediator is needed.

A result of Adam and Eve's sin was that they were removed from direct contact with God. An intermediary or go-between was now needed to bridge the gap. Jesus would be that person but before he could appear God needed to prepare mankind for the full revelation.

A priest was needed. To be qualified to bridge the communication gap, the priest must represent God to man as well as man to God. Only one who combined in his person both divinity and humanity could meet that need. Thus, Jesus as Son of God was born perfectly God in nature, but also perfectly man. Well - almost. Even the Son of God could not represent man to the Father unless he had first personally experienced life lived within the limitations of a human body. His encounters with Satan, his experience of dealing with every temptation that is common to man yet not sinning, and his struggles to submit his will to the Father's will, all brought him to that perfection of experience which may be attained only through suffering. Thus he became qualified to represent man to God, and to represent God to man with all the understanding and compassion of one who had been through it all himself first. This was a vital part of his preparation for priesthood.

> *He had to be made like his brothers in every way, in order that he might become a merciful and faithful high priest in service to God, and that he might make atonement for the sins of the people. (Hebrews 2:17)*

> *For we do not have a high priest who is unable to sympathise with our weaknesses, but we have one who has been tempted in every way, just as we are—yet was without sin.*
> *Let us then approach the throne of grace with confidence, so that we may receive mercy and find grace to help us in our time of need. (Hebrews 4:15-16)*

FIGURE 1
The Tabernacle with the tribes of Israel camped around it.
(from 'Lectures on the Tabernacle'. S. Ridout, Loizeau Brothers, New Lersey, USA 1914.)

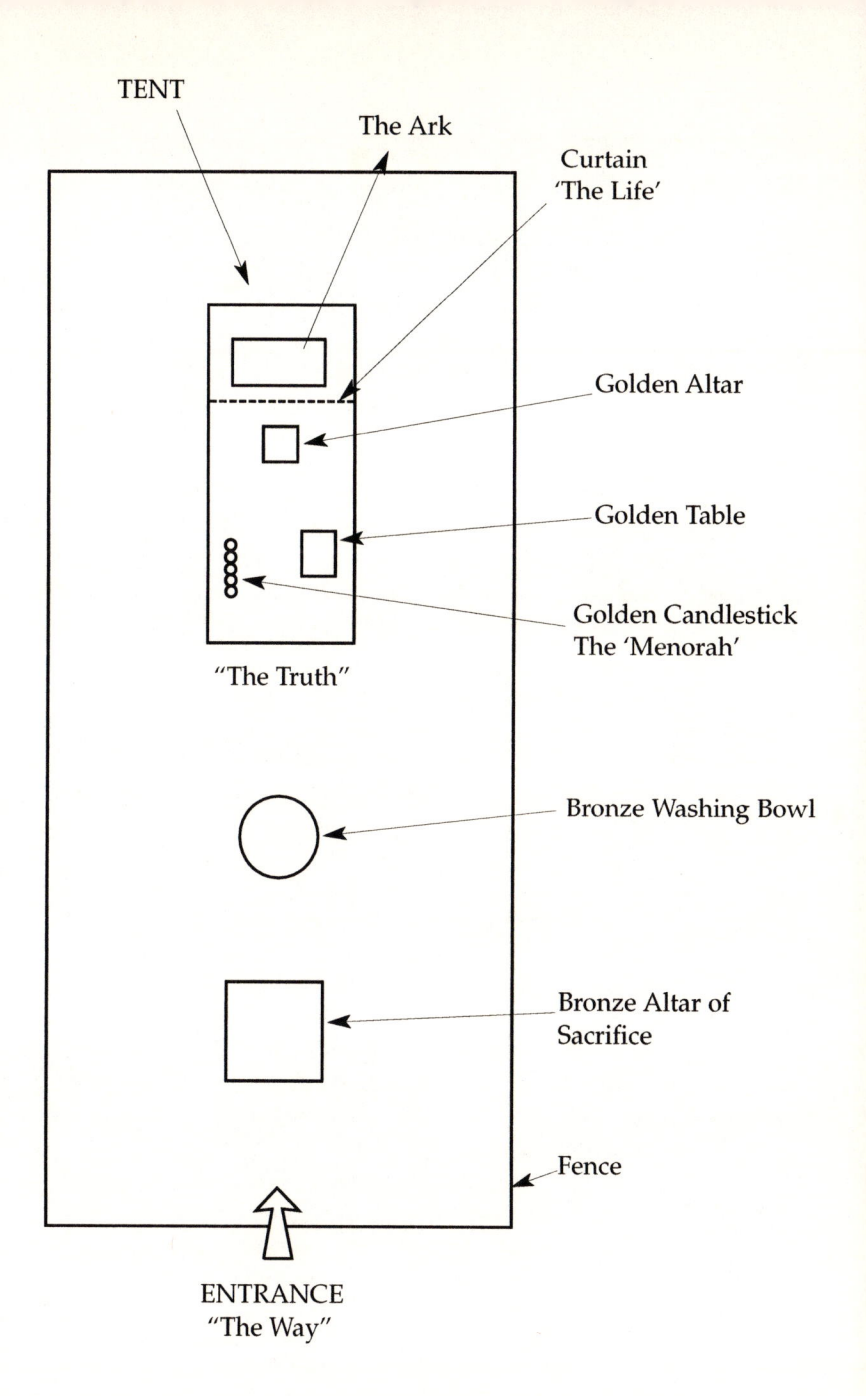

FIGURE 2
The Tabernacle

Jesus' ministry prefigured.

Before Jesus could be born into this world, much preparation was needed. During those many centuries God dropped hints as to the nature of the One who would restore the God-man relationship. Those hints often took the form of individuals whose lives foreshadowed some aspect of Christ's ministry. We can see why. To restore fellowship with man God needed to deal with four things. Provision was needed: (1) for dealing with the sin which separated him from God; and (2) to save man from the curses put upon him as a result his sin, otherwise there was no way he could fellowship with a holy God. Then, (3) the way into Eden, now closed and barred, had to be re-opened and, (4) once the way was opened, man would need help to relate to the God from whom he had been separated for so long. God used the lives of four men in particular to demonstrate these things.

Moses led Israel out of slavery in Egypt, an event that prefigured the salvation from slavery to sin that would come through Christ. Through Moses God began to reveal more about how he was to be approached (the tabernacle) just as Jesus would perfectly reveal the Father to men. God also provided supernaturally through Moses for the daily needs of the Israelis for food and water, just as Jesus would feed thousands from almost nothing whilst declaring himself to be the bread of life.

Moses was assisted by his brother **Aaron**, soon to be designated as High Priest. In that office he would enter the Most Holy Place annually with an offering of the blood of a spotless bull to make atonement for the sins of the nation. Aaron's ministry of atonement was, however, seriously deficient in that it dealt only with unintentional sins, with no provision for the more serious deliberate sins of the heart, and it had to be repeated annually. This limited act of atonement nevertheless prefigured what Christ would do in entering heaven with the ultimate offering of his own blood, thereby sweeping away the need for further Aaronic acts of atonement, and making redundant the entire physical tabernacle or temple.

Together, Moses and Aaron foreshadowed Christ's earthly ministry. Through Jesus salvation came to those who heard him and believed in him. He forgave sins, though only those of the few who came to him, and he himself throughout his life fellowshipped with the Father in the intimacy implied by the Most Holy Place. Glorious as Jesus' earthly ministry was, it alone was not enough to bring man back into intimate fellowship with the Father. A heavenly aspect was also needed because God is Spirit.

Joshua led the way into the promised land. Salvation alone is not enough: we are saved so that we may enter into and enjoy unclouded fellowship with God (the 'promised land') and serve him in the power of the Holy Spirit. Joshua's conquests and occupation of Canaan prefigured Christ's defeat of Satan and subsequent entry into heaven, of which the Most Holy Place is the shadow, shedding and bearing his own blood as the ultimate sacrifice for the sins of the world, thereby opening that way permanently for all believers. But even that is not enough. Given that the way is open, man still needs help in relating to the God from whom he has been separated for so long. After all, a citizen given the opportunity to visit a King or President is advised of the protocol. How much more when God is involved! This is why the ministry of **Melchizedek** is needed.

The rules that confined the Aaronic priesthood were there because it was intended only as a 'shadow' of the priesthood of Jesus. It pointed the way to and the need for something far greater. Therefore, Jesus could not be a Levitical priest or he would have been constrained by the same laws as Aaron. He had to be born in a different tribe. Why Judah? Certainly because that was God's sovereign choice, but that said, there were pointers. Thus, Jacob's deathbed prophecy over Judah, which pre-dated inauguration of the priesthood by about half a millennium:

> *"Judah, your brothers will praise you; your hand will be on the neck of your enemies; your father's sons will bow down to you. You are a lion's cub, O Judah ..... The scepter will not depart from Judah, nor the ruler's staff from between his feet, until he comes to whom it belongs and the*

obedience of the nations is his". (Genesis 49:8-10)

Caleb of Judah was notable for his courage and perseverance in the conquest of Canaan under Joshua, and Judah was the first tribe to anoint David, one of their own, as king in succession to Saul. Thus, the hand of God is seen to be upon the tribe of Judah, Christ's earthly progenitors.

For many centuries then, even before Jacob and his tribe went down to Egypt to escape famine, the scope and nature of Christ's ministry was already revealed. His priesthood is patterned on the mysterious figure of Melchizedek. Like a comet in a hyperbolic orbit, the priest-king Melchizedek appears in scripture in a single close encounter with Abraham, never to be heard of again.

> *This Melchizedek was king of Salem and priest of God Most High. He met Abraham returning from the defeat of the kings and blessed him, and Abraham gave him a tenth of everything. First, his name means "king of righteousness"; then also, "king of Salem" means "king of peace." Without father or mother, without genealogy, without beginning of days or end of life, like the Son of God he remains a priest forever. (Hebrews 7:1-3)*

The differences between the priesthoods of Aaron and Melchizedek translate us directly from the OT to Acts. Whereas the Aaronic priest had to be physically without defect and sexually pure *(Leviticus 21)*, Christ was morally pure and therefore able to defeat Satan, utterly destroying all his work, disarming demonic powers, and setting God's people free from their fear of death.

Moreover, whereas the Aaronic priest was permitted to bless the people, Melchizedek not only blessed Abraham but also brought out bread and wine *(Genesis 14:18)*, foreshadowing Christ's institution of the eucharist (from the Greek *eucharisteo* = to give thanks), a symbolic rite intended to keep fresh the memory of Christ's sacrifice of himself as our Passover lamb *(1 Corinthians 5:7)*, and his offering of his own blood as the final, all-sufficient act of atonement.

A new law.
Aaron ministered within a God-given legal framework. Righteousness was defined as keeping the law *(Deuteronomy 6:25)*. Although the law, coming from God, was holy and good, no-one was able to keep it fully. Thus, the law (1) revealed what God regarded as sin and, (2) since no-one could keep it, pointed up the need for a saviour from sin. Hence, Aaron's ministry as High Priest was of limited efficacy because of the law by which he was confined. The conclusion is obvious: with Jesus as our High Priest after the pattern of Melchizedek there must come also a new law, one which will not restrict his ministry. *When there is a change of the priesthood, there must also be a change of the law (Hebrews 7:12).*

> *For it is declared: "You are a priest forever, in the order of Melchizedek." The former regulation is set aside because it was weak and useless (for the law made nothing perfect), and a better hope is introduced, by which we draw near to God. (Hebrews 7:17-19)*

The entire Law of Moses, the Torah, with its 613 commandments, was rendered obsolete by Jesus' death. It is replaced by the royal law of love, for love is the fulfillment of the Law of Moses.

> *He who loves his fellow man has fulfilled the law. (Romans 13:8)*

Under the New Covenant righteousness is no longer attained, it is obtained by faith in Jesus Christ *(Romans 1:17; 3 : 21-24)*. Praise God for his boundless mercy and grace to us!

Jesus our High Priest.
Moses and Aaron prefigured Jesus' ministry on earth, a work that was completed in every respect. Hence, the cry from the cross: "It is finished!" In contrast, Joshua and Melchizedek imply Jesus' ministry in heavenly places. Part of that is also completed in

that the way into the throne room of heaven is now opened to all believers, but there remains a continuing aspect in that Jesus as our High Priest is there to assist us in our fellowship with the Father.

God's purpose in sending Jesus was to open to us an intimate personal relationship with himself in this present life, as well as for eternity. The torn veil in the Temple is symbolic of the new and living way opened for us through the curtain, that is his body *(Hebrews 10:20)*, made possible by his offering of his own life blood to the Father in heaven. This way has been opened so that we may use it. The tabernacle, the visual aid, is no more. The reality is here: access to the presence of God within the heart of every believer such as even the prophets could not have imagined.

We are to enter the Most Holy Place as did Jesus, namely by obedience and self-sacrifice. In other words, there is a cost - to the flesh. Repentance is turning from sin towards God. The new and living way is turning from the world, separating ourselves to God in order to draw near to him. The pattern is Abraham in his willingness to leave all and set out he knew not where, and Christ in his self-sacrifice.

1.
Jesus, to Thee we fly
On Thee for help rely
Thou our only refuge art
Thou dost all our fears control
Rest of every troubled heart
Life of every dying soul.

2.
We lift our joyful eyes
And see the dazzling prize
See the purchase of Thy blood
Freely now to sinners given
Thou the living way hast showed
Thou to us hast opened heaven.

Seeking The Lord

3.
We now, divinely bold
Of Thy reward lay hold
All Thy glorious joy is ours
All the treasures of Thy love
Now we taste the heavenly powers
Now we reign with Thee above.

4.
Our anchor sure and fast
Within the veil is cast
Stands our never-failing hope
Grounded in the holy place
We shall after Thee mount up
See the Godhead face to face.

Charles Wesley (1707-88)

Chapter 3

Meeting With God

Seeking the Lord.

Jesus said that *"no-one comes to the Father except through me" (John 14:6).* To 'come to the Father' means much more than initial salvation. The whole burden of those aspects of his self-revelation which invite comparison with items of the tabernacle furniture is that only in the person of Jesus is the reality of it experienced. Moreover, the tearing of the temple curtain as he died on the cross, and the grand design of God's sustained passion for his creation, show that he intends his people to seek his face.

Thus, to 'seek the Lord' is not just an OT practice which trickles over into the NT: Jesus died to make it possible for all believers to rise to new heights of intimacy with the Father, limited only by the price they are prepared to pay in dealing with the flesh life. It is the Father's will that we do so.

Without faith it is impossible to please God, because

*anyone who comes to him must believe that he exists
and that he rewards those who earnestly seek him.
(Hebrews 11:6)*

Jesus commanded us to *"Seek first his kingdom and his righteousness"*. *(Matthew 6:33)* To seek the kingdom is to submit to the rule of God, to allow the indwelling Spirit of Jesus to direct our ways. In the course of teaching about the gift of the Holy Spirit, Jesus said:

"So I say to you: Ask and it will be given to you; seek and you will find; knock and the door will be opened to you. For everyone who asks receives; he who seeks finds; and to him who knocks, the door will be opened." (Luke 11:9-10)

The words.
Both the Hebrew and the Greek words in scripture that are translated into English as 'seek' imply a strongly-motivated activity of the heart, a compelling reason to pursue and to search out God's presence. There is nothing lukewarm or half-hearted about it. *Hosea 6:3* catches the sense well: *Let us acknowledge the Lord; let us **press on** to acknowledge him.* And *Isaiah 64:7* its converse: *No-one calls on your name or **strives** to lay hold of you.* The Apostle Paul advises: *Never be lacking in zeal, but keep your **spiritual fervour**, serving the Lord (Romans 12:11).* This is not 'works' any more than it is when two lovers go to any necessary lengths to be together. It is a heart issue.

With all my heart.
I have sought your face with all my heart. (Psalm 119:58)

The scriptures leave no doubt that we are to relate to God wholeheartedly. The biblical concept of the heart is far wider than that of the physical organ that pumps blood. To those who penned the scriptures, the heart is the centre of life, both physically and spiritually; the seat of one's personality, the place of one's entire mental and moral activity. The heart governs and reigns over the whole bodily organism. It includes both rational and emotional elements, but much else besides. It embraces in effect everything that comprises what we call a person

> "The heart is above all the central place in man to
> which God turns, where religious experience has its
> root, and which determines conduct." (E.C. Blackman) [1]

This usage of the term 'heart' is common to both OT and NT. However, the NT is ambivalent in that it also speaks of man as having a three-fold nature: spirit, soul and body, thereby reflecting and updating respectively the Holy of Holies, the Holy Place, and the Outer Court of the tabernacle/temple.

There is no conflict between these two descriptions of man's nature: both are true and both are needed. The same can be said of other pairs of concepts which must be held together, such as time and eternity, or predestination and freewill. Intimacy with God may be spoken of in either framework. Thus, Theophan the Recluse, a Russian Orthodox monk, writing from more than a little experience of seeking the Lord:[2]

> "The physical body is alive because it is endowed
> with a living soul. Into this soul is breathed a
> spirit, intended to know God, to reverence him, to
> seek and taste him, to have its joy in him and
> nothing else."

> "The soul exists primarily on the natural plane.
> The spirit brings us into contact with divine realities:
> it is the highest faculty in man, that which enables
> him to enter into communion with God. To this end
> man's spirit is linked with the Holy Spirit."

> "The body knows through the five senses; the soul
> through intellectual reasoning; the spirit
> through the conscience and through a mystical
> perception that transcends man's ordinary
> rational processes."

So long as we seek God with the intellect alone we shall never encounter him. At best we may know *about* God, but we shall not *know* God. God is spirit, and spirit cannot be comprehended by mere flesh. Therefore, God is beyond reason. He thinks and acts in ways wholly other than ours *(Isaiah 55:9)*. To seek God it is necessary to descend from the head to the heart, but this is not to abandon intellect: reason also is a gift of God

The intellect provides the platform of knowledge and understanding from which we launch out into the depths of God. However, there can be no direct knowedge of God without love of him. That love must come from the whole of our being, from the heart.

> *I belong to my lover, and his desire is for me. Come, my lover, let us go to the countryside, let us spend the night in the villages. Let us go early to the vineyards to see if the vines have budded, if their blossoms have opened,*
> *and if the pomegranates are in bloom— there I will give you my love. (Song of Songs 7:10-12)*

You will find me.

In the OT God promised that those who sought him would find him, and that he himself would be their reward and inheritance.

> *But if .. you seek the LORD your God, you will find him if you look for him with all your heart and with all your soul.(Deuteronomy 4:29)*

> *I love those who love me, and those who seek me find me. (Proverbs 8:17)*

> *You will seek me and find me when you seek me with all your heart. (Jeremiah 29:13)*

> *Blessed are they who keep his statutes, and seek him with all their heart. (Psalm 119:2)*

It is plain from the passionate writings of those who took such invitations seriously, that they were rewarded.

> *One thing I ask of the LORD, this is what I seek: that
> I may dwell in the house of the LORD all the days of my
> life, to gaze upon the beauty of the LORD and to seek him
> in his temple. (Psalm 27:4)*

> *My heart says of you, "Seek his face!" Your face, LORD,
> I will seek. (Psalm 27:8)*

> *O God, you are my God, earnestly I seek you; my soul thirsts
> for you, my body longs for you, in a dry and weary land
> where there is no water. (Psalm 63:1)*

> *How lovely is your dwelling place, O LORD Almighty!
> My soul yearns, even faints, for the courts of the LORD;
> my heart and my flesh cry out for the living God.
> (Psalm 84:1-2)*

> *I will search for the one my heart loves.
> (Song of Songs 3:2)*

> *My soul yearns for you in the night; in the morning
> my spirit longs for you. (Isaiah 26:9)*

You will meet with me.

In those OT days *the Spirit had not been given, since Jesus had not yet been glorified (John 7:39)*. Nevertheless, God rewarded their seeking in a manner that foreshadowed Pentecost, although it seems that those blessings were restricted mainly to prophets and kings. The Spirit was with them rather than in them.

Now, since Pentecost, the situation is dramatically altered. The believer is nothing less than a partaker in the divine nature since Christ lives in him. Moreover, an entirely new way of access into the Father's presence has been opened by Christ's sacrifice. Therefore, as Israel was commanded to 'seek the Lord', so the church is not only to seek him but, astonishingly, also to expect to meet with him!

> *"He made the entire human race and made the earth
> hospitable, with plenty of time and space for living so
> we could seek after God, and not just grope around in
> the dark but actually find him. He doesn't play hide and
> seek with us. He's not remote: he's near."*
> *(Acts 17:26-27 The Message)*

This is to be our expectation as we worship, pray and seek his face. In fact, this is the central burden of *Hebrews*, the book which, more than any other in the NT translates the 'shadow' of Moses' teaching on our approach to God into the reality of the church's new situation.

The context in which the epistle was written further emphasises the significance of our theme in this book. It was directed to a church in poor spiritual condition. They were a generation down the track from Pentecost. They had lost their edge, their zeal, fallen away from the truth. Some had even given up meeting. The godly advice of *Psalm 78:4* had been ignored: *we will tell the next generation.*

The prescription for their ills was to re-focus their understanding on the astonishing intimacy of fellowship which is ours with Christ, if only we will enter into it. Three truths are highlighted:

> 1. Christ has provided a new and living way into the Father's presence.
> 2. We are to enter God's presence by the same way he did, the way of obedience and self-sacrifice.
> 3. There, Christ himself, in his office of eternal High Priest, meets with us.

This is the highest point of revelation in the epistle, which has as its theme the pre-eminence of Christ over every other name or power that can be named. Christ's high priestly office, and our function as priests created to minister to God, stand revealed as the very pinnacle of communion between God and man on earth. Whilst many appreciate that Christ's sacrifice has won for us forgiveness of sins, and that he is our Saviour from sin and death, relatively few understand the significance of meeting with him in his high priestly role.

In the light of these brilliant spiritual truths which have so gripped the writer of *Hebrews*, he issues a warning (one of five in the book):

> *How much more severely do you think a man deserves to be punished who has trampled the Son of God under foot, who has treated as an unholy thing the blood of the covenant that sanctified him, and who has insulted the Spirit of grace? (Hebrews 10:29)*

The way to intimate fellowship with God is wide open. How can we take such a thing lightly? How can we neglect that which Christ died to make freely available to all who love him? This is the solid food of the mature in Christ who are no longer content to remain mere 'infants' in the things of God. This is the open secret of 'abiding' in him: to seek his face and to meet with him. Seeking the Lord is about a deliberate, wholehearted, passionate and insistent approach to God that will not be denied. It is about spending quality time with him for himself alone, and about learning to live in the Most Holy Place.

Whilst this may well be part of our daily life with Christ, the fact remains that God always responds with especial blessings when we set aside longer periods of time for no other reason than to seek his face. It is his joy that it's our joy. Again, we may do this individually or corporately. The emphasis of the practical comments in this study is upon the corporate aspect, because this is such an effective way of deepening a whole church in their experience of and walk with God.

CHAPTER 4

Why Seek God?

The aim of this Chapter is to let the scriptures speak to us about why we are to seek God, and about the blessings that follow in consequence.

It's what he wants and commands.

> *The LORD looks down from heaven on the sons of men to see if there are any who understand, any who seek God. (Psalm 14:2 & 53:2)*

> *"I love those who love me, and those who seek me find me." (Proverbs 8:17)*

Seek first his kingdom and his righteousness (Matthew 6:33)

And without faith it is impossible to please God, because anyone who comes to him must believe that he exists and that he rewards those who earnestly seek him. (Hebrews 11:6)

After this I looked, and there before me was a door standing open in heaven. And the voice I had first heard speaking to me like a trumpet said, "Come up here, and I will show you what must take place after this." At once I was in the Spirit, and there before me was a throne in heaven with someone sitting on it. (Revelation 4:1-2)

To allow him to search our hearts.

It is always time to seek the Lord, but especially so when we have become lukewarm, lost our first love, run out of zeal, find that our prayer life is dull and unrewarding, or that our meetings have lost their edge and become routine.

God loathes lukewarmness so much that he actually prefers coldness of heart *(Revelation 3:15-16)*. To be lukewarm is to be contemptuous of God, to treat the benefits of Christ's passion as of little value compared with the things of the flesh. It means that either our heart never was in fact given to God and that we are living in self-deception, or that we have allowed the living sacrifice to crawl off the altar. Then, the only way forward is by repentance.

"In those days, at that time," declares the LORD,
"the people of Israel and the people of Judah together
will go in tears to seek the LORD their God." (Jeremiah 50:4)

Then I will go back to my place until they admit their guilt. And they will seek my face; in their misery they will earnestly seek me." (Hosea 5:15)

This is what the LORD says: "Cursed is the one who trusts in man, who depends on flesh for his strength and whose heart turns away from the LORD. .... The heart is deceitful above

Why Seek God?

> *all things and beyond cure. Who can understand it?"*
> *I the LORD search the heart and examine the mind,*
> *to reward a man according to his conduct, according to*
> *what his deeds deserve." (Jeremiah 17:5,9-10)*

> *Search me, O God, and know my heart; test me and*
> *know my anxious thoughts. See if there is any offensive*
> *way in me, and lead me in the way everlasting.*
> *(Psalm 139:23-24)*

> *The sacrifices of God are a broken spirit; a broken*
> *and contrite heart, O God, you will not despise. (Psalm 51:17)*

> *"This is the one I esteem: he who is humble and contrite*
> *in spirit, and trembles at my word." (Isaiah 66:2)*

As we humble ourselves before God he will sometimes show us things in our heart of which we were unaware. Others may well have seen them too, but to us they are news. It is important, therefore, to approach the throne of grace in complete openness, and not just with an agenda of things we perceive as needing attention.

To build a personal relationship with him through intimate fellowship.

We are assured that God will respond to our seeking him, and that we shall 'find' him. But it must be a wholehearted and passionate seeking.

> *"But if ... you seek the LORD your God, you will find him*
> *if you look for him with all your heart and with*
> *all your soul." (Deuteronomy 4:29)*

> *"And you, my son Solomon, acknowledge the God of*
> *your father, and serve him with wholehearted devotion*
> *and with a willing mind, for the LORD searches every*
> *heart and understands every motive behind the thoughts.*
> *If you seek him, he will be found by you; but if you forsake him,*
> *he will reject you forever." (1 Chronicles 28:9)*

*He [the prophet Azariah] went out to meet Asa and said to him,
"Listen to me, Asa and all Judah and Benjamin.
The LORD is with you when you are with him. If you seek him,
he will be found by you, but if you forsake him,
he will forsake you...".
They entered into a covenant to seek the LORD,
the God of their fathers, with all their heart and soul.
(2 Chronicles 15:2 & 12)*

*I seek you with all my heart; do not let me stray
from your commands. (Psalm 119:10)*

*"You will seek me and find me when you seek me
with all your heart." (Jeremiah 29:13)*

*"Even now," declares the LORD, "return to me with all
your heart, with fasting and weeping and mourning."
(Joel 2:12)*

"Let everyone call urgently on God." (Jonah 3:8)

*"Ask and it will be given to you; seek and you will find;
knock and the door will be opened to you." (Matthew 7:7)*

*And without faith it is impossible to please God,
because anyone who comes to him must believe that he
exists and that he rewards those who earnestly seek him.
(Hebrews 11:6)*

To seek his counsel, wisdom and guidance, especially when motivated by distress.

*But Jehoshaphat also said to the king of Israel, "First seek
the counsel of the LORD." (1 Kings 22:5 & 2 Chronicles 18:4)*

*But Jehoshaphat asked, "Is there not a prophet of the LORD
here whom we can inquire of?" (1 Kings 22:7)*

*Alarmed, Jehoshaphat resolved to inquire of the LORD,
and he proclaimed a fast for all Judah. (2 Chronicles 20:3)*

*Then Jehoahaz sought the Lord's favour, and the LORD
listened to him, for he saw how severely the king of Aram
was oppressing Israel. (2 Kings 13:4)*

*But in their distress they [King Asa and all Judah] turned
to the LORD, the God of Israel, and sought him, and he was
found by them. (2 Chronicles 15:4)*

*The people of Judah [under King Jehoshaphat] came together
to seek help from the LORD; indeed, they came from every town
in Judah to seek him. (2 Chronicles 20:4)*

*In his distress he [King Manasseh of Judah] sought the favour
of the LORD his God and humbled himself greatly before
the God of his fathers. And when he prayed to him, the LORD
was moved by his entreaty and listened to his plea; so he brought
him back to Jerusalem and to his kingdom. Then Manasseh knew
that the LORD is God . (2 Chronicles 33:12-13).*

*"When I was in distress, I sought the Lord; at night
I stretched out untiring hands and my soul refused
to be comforted." (Psalm 77:2)*

*"Cover their faces with shame so that men will seek
your name, O LORD." (Psalm 83:16)*

*He said: "In my distress I called to the LORD, and he
answered me. From the depths of the grave I called
for help, and you listened to my cry." (Jonah 2:2)*

*"And many peoples and powerful nations will come
to Jerusalem to seek the LORD Almighty and to entreat him."
(Zechariah 8:22)*

In trial and distress we glimpse a deeper, a disturbing, force at work. All our circumstances, however puzzling, even malign, they may seem to be, are orchestrated with one end in view: to cause us to seek God *(cf. Acts 17:26-28)*. He is in "the slings and arrows of outrageous fortune" as well as the blessings. Strangely however, there seems to be little direct correlation between the way we live our lives, and the things that happen to us. Therefore, we are to seek his face, and to enquire of him, because to stand *in the council of the Lord to see or to hear his word (Jeremiah 23:18,22)* is to receive supernatural wisdom and guidance. This too is part of the fruit of seeking his face.

> *The babies jostled each other within her, and she said, "Why is this happening to me?" So she went to inquire of the LORD. (Genesis 25:22)*
>
> *Then they said to him, "Please inquire of God to learn whether our journey will be successful." (Judges 18:5)*
>
> *Once again David inquired of the LORD, and the LORD answered him, "Go down to Keilah, for I am going to give the Philistines into your hand." (1 Samuel 23:4)*
>
> *David inquired of the LORD, "Shall I pursue this raiding party? Will I overtake them?" "Pursue them," he answered. "You will certainly overtake them and succeed in the rescue." (1 Samuel 30:8)*
>
> *In the course of time, David inquired of the LORD. "Shall I go up to one of the towns of Judah?" he asked. The LORD said, "Go up." David asked, "Where shall I go?" "To Hebron," the LORD answered. (2 Samuel 2:1)*
>
> *David inquired of the LORD, "Shall I go and attack the Philistines? Will you hand them over to me?" The LORD answered him, "Go, for I will surely hand the Philistines over to you." (2 Samuel 5:19)*
>
> *During the reign of David, there was a famine for three successive years; so David sought the face of the LORD. The LORD said, "It is on account of Saul and his*

Why Seek God?

*blood-stained house; it is because he put the
Gibeonites to death." (2 Samuel 21:1)*

*"When men tell you to consult mediums and spiritists,
who whisper and mutter, should not a people inquire
of their God? Why consult the dead on behalf of the living?"
(Isaiah 8:19)*

*"Inquire now of the LORD for us because Nebuchadnezzar
king of Babylon is attacking us. Perhaps the LORD will perform
wonders for us as in times past so that he will withdraw
from us." (Jeremiah 21:2)*

*"In the seventh year, in the fifth month on the tenth day,
some of the elders of Israel came to inquire of the LORD,
and they sat down in front of me." (Ezekiel 20:1)*

Benefits of seeking God.

In addition to the incomparable blessings of meeting with our Lord in the Most Holy Place, of hearing his voice and receiving guidance and direction, the anointing upon us increases as we come into greater obedience to him. He is then able to use us in ever more powerful ways. Moreover:

The life and joy of the Lord are ours.

*The poor will eat and be satisfied; they who seek the
LORD will praise him— may your hearts live forever!
(Psalm 22:26)*

*But may all who seek you rejoice and be glad in you;
may those who love your salvation always say,
"The LORD be exalted!" (Psalm 40:16 & 70:4)*

*The poor will see and be glad— you who seek God,
may your hearts live! (Psalm 69:32)*

*Glory in his holy name; let the hearts of those who
seek the LORD rejoice. (1 Chronicles 16:10 & Psalm 105:3)*

This is what the LORD says to the house of Israel:
"Seek me and live". (Amos 5:4)

The life and joy which are ours in him are not for ourselves alone, but that we may be light and salt to the world, and so that we may minister more effectively to others. The more we receive, the more we have to give. *We love because he first loved us (1 John 4:19).* Our personal and ongoing experience of the love of God as we seek his face enables us to love even the unlovely with the love that is in Christ Jesus.

We are strengthened and blessed.

"Look to the LORD and his strength; seek his face always."
(1 Chronicles 16:11 & Psalm 105:4)

"I sought the LORD, and he answered me; he delivered me from all my fears." (Psalm 34:4)

"The lions may grow weak and hungry, but those who seek the LORD lack no good thing." (Psalm 34:10)

Blessed are they who keep his statutes and seek him with all their heart. ... I will walk about in freedom, for I have sought out your precepts. (Psalm 119:2 & 45)

"Sharon will become a pasture for flocks, and the Valley of Achor a resting place for herds, for my people who seek me." (Isaiah 65:10)

For there is no difference between Jew and Gentile—
the same Lord is Lord of all and richly blesses
all who call on him, (Romans 10:12)

The church is blessed and enriched by the worship and the prayers of those who dwell in his presence. They are able to 'lift' the whole spiritual temperature, to act like the tip of an arrow, so that others may follow more easily into intimacy with God.

Why Seek God?

We, the church, and the nation are prospered.

When God is central to our life, we and our families are prospered, but the blessings are far wider than that. Each Christian household should be a neighbourhood prayer watch, bringing God's peace and presence to those about them. Likewise, each church has a region of spiritual influence, usually a geographical area around its building, although in the case of strategic churches the whole city is affected. Just as sin is a social disease (because sin is always against someone), so also righteousness is a social phenomenon with associated blessings that extend far beyond ourselves.

The nation is blessed as godly people seek his face, as is shown dramatically by some of the following scriptures. National days of prayer in Britain during the second world war yielded amazing results, as even secular historians admit.

> *"If my people, who are called by my name, will humble themselves and pray and seek my face and turn from their wicked ways, then will I hear from heaven and will forgive their sin and will heal their land." (2 Chronicles 7:14)*

> *"Let us build up these towns," he [King Asa] said to Judah, "and put walls around them, with towers, gates and bars. The land is still ours, because we have sought the LORD our God; we sought him and he has given us rest on every side." So they built and prospered. (2 Chronicles 14:7)*

> *All Judah rejoiced about the oath because they had sworn it wholeheartedly. They sought God eagerly, and he was found by them. So the LORD gave them rest on every side. (2 Chronicles 15:15)*

> *He [Uzziah of Judah] sought God during the days of Zechariah, who instructed him in the fear of God. As long as he sought the LORD, God gave him success. (2 Chronicles 26:5)*

> *In everything that he [Hezekiah] undertook in the service*

of God's temple and in obedience to the law and the commands,
he sought his God and worked wholeheartedly.
And so he prospered. (2 Chronicles 31:21)
"Did not Hezekiah fear the LORD and seek his favour?
And did not the LORD relent, so that he did not bring
the disaster he pronounced against them?"
(Jeremiah 26:19)

God's purpose for his world is to restore to it Eden-like life. He is doing this through the church, to whom he has delegated all authority for that purpose. Hence, while seeking the Lord undoubtedly begins on a personal level, it extends also to increasing degrees of corporate action, to church and even nation. Seeking the Lord is, therefore, scale-invariant.

Consequences of not seeking the Lord.

Not seeking God brings fearsome consequences. *My people are destroyed from lack of knowledge (Hosea 4:6)*. The wider context is that of *Deuteronomy 28*. As we keep the Lord's commands, including the injunction to seek his face, we automatically bring our lives under his blessing. The converse, a very long list of disasters, follows from disobedience. Scriptures such as those below remain relevant to us, for we too may have idols in our lives, and above all, self-will.

> *Saul died because he was unfaithful to the LORD;*
> *he did not keep the word of the LORD and even consulted*
> *a medium for guidance, and did not inquire of the LORD.*
> *So the LORD put him to death and turned the kingdom*
> *over to David son of Jesse. (1 Chronicles 10:13-14)*

> *They abandoned the temple of the LORD, the God of*
> *their fathers, and worshiped Asherah poles and idols.*
> *Because of their guilt, God's anger came upon Judah*
> *and Jerusalem. (2 Chronicles 24:18)*

> *"I will scatter you like chaff driven by the desert wind.*
> *This is your lot, the portion I have decreed for you,"*
> *declares the LORD, "because you have forgotten me and*

trusted in false gods." (Jeremiah 13:24-25)

"Just as it is written in the Law of Moses, all this disaster has come upon us, yet we have not sought the favour of the LORD our God by turning from our sins and giving attention to your truth." (Daniel 9:13)

"I will stretch out my hand against Judah and against all who live in Jerusalem. I will cut off from this place every remnant of Baal, the names of the pagan and the idolatrous priests ..... those who turn back from following the LORD and neither seek the LORD nor inquire of him." (Zephaniah 1:4,6)

Thus:

Seeking the Lord is not an optional extra indulged in by a particular type of church stream. It is intended by God to be a central aspect of our life in him.

Marriage is the model.

God speaks in scripture of marriage as a model for our relationship to himself (Chapter 1). It is a commonplace in marriage guidance circles to advise couples to spend quality time together to keep their marriage healthy. Why? Basically, for the same reasons we are to seek God. After all, marriage partners were joined in the first place because of a desire to be with each other for life. Communication is one of the key issues in marriage, in defusing problem situations, in reaching decisions, and in getting to know each other at a deeper level.

This is a good starting attitude for seeking God, but let us be careful to add to it *the fear of the Lord,* for that is the beginning of wisdom. Intimacy must be balanced with awesomeness in the presence of the Living God.

Chapter 5

Behold Your God

By faith.
We seek God's face, and meet with him in the Most Holy Place, by faith. Faith invariably rests upon what God has said. Therefore, as we approach him, it is important to know and understand what God has said about himself, and to be sure that what we believe about him agrees with what he has said. Doctrinal faith is the basis of living faith.

God's character.
Everything known about God has come by way of his self-revelation. His character is like a many-faceted jewel. Its totality is awesome in wonder and beauty. We shall prepare ourselves for seeking his face by looking briefly at some of the key biblical words

used of God. It is important to be utterly convinced that he is love, that his mercy never fails, and neither does his patience, that he is gracious beyond all imagining, for if we do not believe these things we shall find it hard to relate to him as he is. But first let us understand that over and above all that God has revealed about himself and his intentions there broods this yet more awesome revelation: *I am holy.*

Holiness sums up God's character. It is the collective term for all his attributes - those he has chosen to reveal to man, and those that remain hidden. It is far more than awesomeness allied to moral perfection. White light passed through a prism reveals its constituent colours, yet light in all its subtlety is far more than the sum of its parts. So it is with the holiness of God.

Basically, holiness means 'to be different', set apart from the common and ordinary. To say that God is holy means that he is unique and unlike man in every way. The obvious implication is that we too must be 'different' if we are to relate to him in intimacy.

God's holiness is experienced primarily through his revealed qualities of love, mercy, righteousness, grace, power, glory, and many others. All these qualities are also different from ours of the same names. To each individual he reveals precisely what they are able to receive at that moment. Thus:

> *To the faithful you show yourself faithful, to the blameless you show yourself blameless, to the pure you show yourself pure, but to the crooked you show yourself shrewd.*
> *(Psalm 18:25-26)*

To Moses God could speak of his love and mercy because Moses had already met with him in his holiness at the burning bush. In contrast, to the Israeli people the emphasis of his revelation had to be on a righteousness associated with keeping his laws, because they were to live amongst nations whose religious rites included sexual licence and even child sacrifice. To have spoken to them only of love would not have restrained them and formed them into a holy nation. Therefore, God gave them laws to show *how* to love both him and their neighbour.

As we draw near to God, to seek his face, or even call out to him in distress, he will reveal himself to us with whatever quality is most appropriate to our condition: his fatherhood, love, forgiveness, or perhaps mercy. Like Paul, some may be overwhelmed by his grace.

Relationship is the key.
God's intention is that our relationship with him should develop in depth and intimacy, just as two people who have fallen in love joyfully explore each other's life and character. In this he has an end in view: that we should know him as he is and, because we love him, become like him. Thus, is man prepared by God, through intimacy of loving relationship, to receive the revelation which will be the key to his climbing the heights: *I the LORD am holy.*

> *"You are to be holy to me because I, the LORD, am holy, and I have set you apart from the nations to be my own." (Leviticus 20:26)*

I the LORD am holy.
The first occurrence of the concept of holiness is in *Genesis 2:3. And God blessed the seventh day and made it holy.* That apart, there is no further mention of holiness until God met with Moses at the burning bush. *Take off your sandals for the place where you are standing is holy ground (Exodus 3:5).* By definition, where God is is holy.

The word 'holy' is of very wide occurrence throughout the Bible but it occurs with particular frequency in the Pentateuch which accounts for over 40% of its OT uses. It is found 45 times in Leviticus alone. The conclusion is obvious: God wants his people to grasp the importance of holiness.

The word *qodesh*.
To appreciate something of the meaning of holiness, we need to understand three key Hebrew words that belong to the borderland of the natural with the supernatural. The first is *qodesh*,

which means 'holiness'. Indeed, the word itself is holy. Its' origin in an ancient Semitic language, now lost, is unknown. What is certain is that as it emerges from the mists of prehistory it is found to be reserved exclusively for reference to God, never to man, and specifically to that quality which more than any other defines his being: he is holy.

His holiness is absolute and unique. It cannot be imagined or imitated, earned or acquired. It is the fountainhead from which flow all his other attributes, especially love, mercy, grace and longsuffering. These attributes are displayed and made freely available to us precisely with this end in view: that we may know him in his holiness.

> *This is what the high and lofty One says: he who*
> *lives for ever, whose name is holy: "I live in a high*
> *and holy place, but also with him who is contrite and*
> *lowly in spirit." (Isaiah 57:15).*

The word *cherem*.

Secondly, the word *cherem* is also used among Semitic peoples for that which belongs to the gods. However, to the Hebrews it took a specific meaning. It refers to that which has been qodesh to a god other than Jehovah and which must, therefore, be utterly, completely and ruthlessly destroyed. Indeed, cherem is often translated as 'destroy'. "One god's *qodesh* was another god's *cherem*. The devotees of one god therefore destroyed all they could capture of the other god's property, whether it was animate or inanimate" (N.H. Snaith)[1]. The idea of 'forbidden' is essential to the meaning of *cherem* in a way that is not the case with *qodesh*.

These concepts are well illustrated by **the Jericho campaign** and its sequel, the sin of Achan.

> *"Keep away from the devoted things, so that you will*
> *not bring about your own destruction by taking any of them.*
> *Otherwise you will make the camp of Israel liable to*
> *destruction and bring trouble on it. All the silver and gold*
> *and the articles of bronze and iron are sacred to the LORD*

and must go into his treasury." (Joshua 6:18-19)

They devoted the city [Jericho] to the LORD and destroyed with the sword every living thing in it—men and women, young and old, cattle, sheep and donkeys. (Joshua 6:21)

"Go, consecrate the people. Tell them, 'Consecrate yourselves in preparation for tomorrow; for this is what the LORD, the God of Israel, says: That which is devoted is among you, O Israel. You cannot stand against your enemies until you remove it." (Joshua 7:13)

The word *chol*.
The third word of importance in this context is *chol*, which means 'common or ordinary'. It is everywhere the opposite of both *qodesh* and *cherem*. The root meaning of *qodesh* is 'separation'. God is separate and distinct because he is God. He is unique - there is none like him. *"To whom will you compare me, or who is my equal?" says the Holy One (Isaiah 40:25).* In the same sense, a person or thing may become holy by entering into the conditions that are associated with holiness.

The whole sense is positive. It is not separation from anything or anyone. Rather, the emphasis is on having come into the category of the separate that is distinct from the ordinary or common. Hence the words 'separated to God' more accurately express the meaning as in *Numbers 6:2: "Speak to the Israelites and say to them: 'If a man or woman wants to make a special vow, a vow of separation to the LORD as a Nazirite, ... "* It is not so much separation from anything, because that would lead to an arid legalism. Rather it is separation to God, a heart issue. The same thinking applies to the marriage covenant.

Holiness does not mean remoteness.
The fact that the root meaning of holiness is 'separation' in no way implies that God is remote from his creation - quite the opposite in fact as many of the above instances have shown. He is different from man but intimately involved with him. Thus, *Hosea (11:9): "I am God, and not man— the Holy One among you."* And

supremely so in Jesus.

For us also, holiness does not mean remoteness. We are to be in the world yet not of it. Hear Paul:

> *"Our conscience testifies that we have conducted ourselves*
> *in the world, and especially in our relations with you,*
> *in the holiness and sincerity that are from God."*
> *(2 Corinthians 1:12)*

What is holy?
The first passover (the one in Egypt) is declared holy *(Exodus 12:16)*, and so is the Sabbath *(Exodus 16:23)*. Then God reveals his intention for Israel: *"You will be for me a kingdom of priests and a holy nation."* *(Exodus 19:6)*.

There are, moreover, degrees of holiness associated with the closeness to his presence. In the tabernacle, there is the Holy Place, and the more awesome Most Holy Place where God promised to meet with Moses. The priests are holy, and so even are their garments. The altar, the vessels used in the sanctuary, the offerings made to God, all are declared holy (e.g. *Leviticus 27:22-24,28*). Holiness whether of persons or of things thus involves separation from common use and dedication to a sacred one. **The principle is clear: that which God accepts and graces with his presence becomes holy**, be it a person, an event, or a thing.

Some things are forbidden because they are unclean, others because they have been devoted to God. *"Nothing that a man owns and devotes to the LORD—whether man or animal or family land—may be sold or redeemed; everything so devoted is most holy to the LORD."* *(Leviticus 27:28)*. Moreover, God requires his people to make a clear distinction between the holy and the common.

> *"Her priests do violence to my law and profane my holy things;*
> *they do not distinguish between the holy and the common;*
> *they teach that there is no difference between the unclean and*
> *the clean; and they shut their eyes to the keeping of my Sabbaths,*
> *so that I am profaned among them." (Ezekiel 22:26)*

In the final analysis of human destiny in eternity, there are but two categories - the righteous and the wicked, those who have chosen holiness and those who have rejected it. Thus, the prophet *Malachi (3:18)* speaking of the great and terrible day of the LORD, says that on it *"you will again see the distinction between the righteous and the wicked, between those who serve God and those who do not"*.

God's holy people.

Since God is holy, anything unclean, unsanctified or common (the opposite of holiness) cannot exist in his presence. Therefore, for man to enter his presence, to be in the Most Holy Place, he must himself first be made holy. To the unclean, God's holiness is frightening rather than attractive. Therefore he draws us by his qualities of love, mercy, grace and longsuffering. Once we have responded to his word of truth, been cleansed from sin by Jesus' blood, acknowledged that our 'old man' was nailed to the cross with Christ, and received the promised Holy Spirit - then *"we have confidence to enter the Most Holy Place" (Hebrews 10:19)*.

It is important to understand that God's love is not an end in itself, but one of the means by which he develops in us the desire to be Christ-like. Certainly he draws us in love, but if our focus remains on the love we risk being side-tracked into feelings-centred emotionalism. See his love then, as the means by which he enters our hearts and develops with us an intimate relationship that can only be fully satisfied by seeking him in his holiness.

Our part.

Holiness is of God. Therefore only God can make a person or thing holy. *I am the Lord who makes you holy (Exodus 31:13)*. There is, however, a part played by us. **We are to choose to be holy**, and consistently to reaffirm that choice. Thus:

> *"He chose us in him before the creation of the world to be holy and blameless in his sight." (Ephesians 1:4)*

> *"Therefore, I urge you, brothers, in view of God's mercy, to offer your bodies as living sacrifices, holy and pleasing to God— this is your spiritual act of worship." (Romans 12:1)*

*To the church of God in Corinth, to those sanctified in
Christ Jesus and called to be holy, together with all those
everywhere who call on the name of our Lord Jesus Christ—
their Lord and ours: (1 Corinthians 1:2)*

*"Do you not know that your body is a temple of the
Holy Spirit, who is in you, whom you have received
from God?" (1 Corinthians 6:19)*

*"It is God's will that you should be sanctified: that you
should avoid sexual immorality; that each of you should
learn to control his own body in a way that is holy and
honourable, ... for God did not call us to be impure, but to
live a holy life." (1 Thessalonians 4:3-4,7)*

*"Both the one who makes men holy and those who are
made holy are of the same family. So Jesus is not ashamed
to call them brothers." (Hebrews 2:11)*

*"Our fathers disciplined us for a little while as they
thought best; but God disciplines us for our good,
that we may share in his holiness." (Hebrews 12:10)*

*"Make every effort to live in peace with all men
and to be holy; without holiness no one will
see the Lord." (Hebrews 12:14)*

*"But just as he who called you is holy, so be holy
in all you do for it is written: "Be holy, because I am holy.""
(1 Peter 1:15-16)*

*Worship the Lord in the splendour of his holiness.
(Psalm 96:9)*

God wants his people to grasp the importance of holiness.

According to Christ, those whom he has sanctified *"are not of the world"* (John 17:14).

Chapter 6

God is Love

"God is love" and *"we love because he first loved us" (1John 4:16, 19)*. Along with love we must look at mercy and compassion, as well as grace, because these are closely-related and overlapping concepts.

Love: the words *ahaba* & *agape*.

The Hebrew word *ahaba* is by far the most commonly-used OT word for love. It stands for passionate love between the sexes, but also for family and other ties of affection. In a theological sense it is used of God's love for men, and of men's love for God. *Ahaba* is God's spontaneous and unconditional love, not the response to any worth or attractiveness in its object. It is a love that seeks to serve its object rather than to possess it. *Ahaba* tells us that God loves because his nature is to love. Examples of the use of *ahaba* are:

> *"He has taken me to the banquet hall,
> and his banner over me is love." (Song of Solomon 2:4)*
> *"The Lord appeared to us in the past, saying: "I have loved you
> with an everlasting love; I have drawn you with
> loving-kindness"". (Jeremiah 31:3)*
>
> *"I led them with cords of human kindness, with ties
> of love; I lifted the yoke from their neck and bent down
> to feed them." (Hosea 11:4)*

The Jewish Rabbis who translated the OT scriptures into Greek (the Septuagint) during the second century BC took a little-used Greek word, *agape,* as the direct equivalent of *ahaba. Agape* is a word reserved in scripture exclusively for the love of God for men, and for God's love expressed in and through men. About 90% of all NT references to love use *agape.*

Mercy: the word *chesed.*

In the cluster of terms used to describe God's love, the second most frequently-used Hebrew word is *chesed.* It is translated most commonly as 'mercy' (64%), but also as 'kindness' (22%) or 'loving kindness' (14%). The contexts in which this word is used show that God's mercy arises out of his total commitment to us. God has taken the initiative and has bound himself in a solemn covenant or agreement to love us. Therefore, *chesed* is often referred to as God's 'covenant love'.

The very existence of such a covenant shows the depths of his mercy and loving kindness to us. The covenant is between the Father and the Son, Jesus. Out of his commitment to us Jesus gave his life on the cross so that we may be saved from the death which our sinful nature deserves, and brought into eternal life, a personal, intimate loving relationship with our God who now lives within us by his Spirit. For his part the Father honours the Son's total commitment to us by extending his mercy to us, a mercy which he will never retract under any conditions whatsoever. People may fail us, everything around us may be shaken, the very foundations of society may be torn apart, but God's mercies endure forever.

God Is Love

"Ultimately mercy is God choosing to deal with us, not as we deserve, but as Jesus deserves" (Colin Urquhart).

*"For God so loved the world that he gave his one
and only Son, that whoever believes in him
shall not perish but have eternal life."* (John 3:16)

*"Because of the Lord's great love we are not consumed,
for his compassions never fail.
They are new every morning: great is your faithfulness."*
(Lamentations 3:22-23)

The word *châshaq*.

The root meaning is to cling, be attached to, love and delight in. It is a love which will not let go. Examples:

*"Because he loves me [châshaq]," says the LORD,
"I will rescue him; I will protect him, for he acknowledges
my name. (Psalm 91:14)*

*"Surely it was for my benefit that I suffered such anguish.
In your love [châshaq] you kept me from the pit of destruction;
you have put all my sins behind your back." (Isaiah 38:17)*

Compassion: the word *râcham*.

Compassion is very closely allied to mercy. Indeed the Hebrew word *râcham* is translated sometimes as 'compassion' and sometimes as 'tender mercies'. It's a beautiful word: the root meaning is to fondle, soothe, cherish, love deeply. It refers to a strong love rooted in some natural bond. Small babies may evoke this feeling. Such are God's tender mercies, his compassion. Examples:

*"Can a mother forget the baby at her breast and have no
compassion on the child she has borne? Though she may forget,
I will not forget you!" (Isaiah 49:15)*

*"As a father has compassion on his children, so the LORD
has compassion on those who fear him." (Psalm 103:13)*

The NT Greek word for 'compassion' *(splanchnizomai)* is also very revealing. It is derived from the word for bowels *(splanchnon)*. The old-fashioned phrase 'bowels of mercies' is in fact a very accurate rendering of the true meaning of the term, as witness *1 John 3:17* in the King James Version of the Bible. *But whoso hath this world's good, and seeth his brother have need, and shutteth up his bowels of compassion from him, how dwelleth the love of God in him?* In the gospels we find that Jesus healed the sick out of his compassion, and that that compassion was really a mixture of love plus anger at the work of the devil in that person's life. He does the same today through those who allow his compassion to work in their hearts.

Grace.

> "The idea of grace more than any other idea binds
> the two testaments together into a complete whole,
> for the Bible is the story of the saving work of God,
> that is, of the grace of God. Without grace, there would
> never have been any chosen people, any story to tell at all."
> (N.H. Snaith) [1]

In the OT the Hebrew word *chen* is translated both as 'grace' (60%) and 'favour' (40%). The word implies kindness and goodwill of a superior to an inferior entirely without obligation on the part of the giver. Examples:

> *Joseph found favor [chen] in his [Potiphar's] eyes and became his attendant. (Genesis 39:4)*

> *"He mocks proud mockers but gives grace [chen] to the humble." (Proverbs 3:34)*

> *"And I will pour out on the house of David and the inhabitants of Jerusalem a spirit of grace [chen] and supplication." (Zechariah 12:10)*

In the Septuagint the Hebrew *chen* is rendered into Greek as *charis* = 'grace'. The root meaning of *charis* is 'to be cheerful, joyful, to rejoice'. In the NT charis is of wide occurrence, with Paul alone accounting for 70% of its uses. Overall in the NT, more than one in

God is Love

four uses of *charis* occur in greetings or endings of letters, where the meaning is the same as that in the OT use of *chen*. In a secular sense, when our Queen makes certain living quarters available to her servants, these are termed 'grace and favour' apartments.

However, in Paul's writings especially, the content of *charis* inherited from *chen* was wholly inadequate to express what he, *"the worst of sinners" (1 Timothy 1:16)*, had experienced of the grace of God, which seemed to him to be inextricably tied in with the unfailing covenant love of God. Then why not use the Greek equivalent of *chesed*? The problem here is that the Septuagint Rabbis had translated *chesed* into Greek as *eleos* = pity, which certainly didn't fit the need. The end result of this thinking was that Paul (and others) opted for the Greek word *charis* anyway, but used it in such fashion as to invest it with much of the content of *chesed* as well as that of *chen*. Thus we arrive at the characteristic NT use of the word 'grace' which is of God's freely-given redemptive covenant love towards sinners whom he wants to save and lead into an intimate relationship with him.

"Grace is love reaching down." (Anon)

"Grace is the divine strength working in us."
(Andrew Murray)

"Grace is God giving everything to those who
deserve nothing." (Colin Urquhart)[2]

"Grace describes God's attitude towards the law-breaker
and the rebel; mercy is his attitude toward those who
are in distress." (W.E. Vine)[3]

"Mercy is the entrance into God's grace." (Colin Urquhart)[2]

"Whatever God does by grace is a gift from him and cannot
depend at all on our works. That is why it is so important
to free people from the idea that God will heal them
or meet some need only if they first get their lives
sorted out! What we receive by grace does not depend

on our walk." (Colin Urquhart)[4]

Patience.

Both the Hebrew and Greek words used in this context have the basic meaning 'long'. Thus, the Greek *makrothumia* (from *makros* = long, *thumos* = temper) is usually translated as 'longsuffering' but also as 'patience' or 'slow to anger'. It is part of God's character.

Longsuffering "describes that attitude of God whereby strict justice would long ago have swept Israel away in penalty for her sin and rebellion if it had not been that God is 'slow to anger and of great mercy'" (N.H. Snaith)[1]. It is "that quality of self-restraint in the face of provocation which does not hastily retaliate or promptly punish. It is the opposite of anger, and is associated with mercy" (W.E. Vine)[3].

These precise academic definitions conform fully with our experience. Those who have experienced the mighty grace of God, when looking back cannot fail to be amazed at the patience with which he has dealt with them, and conclude that the motive can only be love of a supernatural order and purpose. The connection between patience and mercy (= covenant love) cannot be doubted and is nowhere more passionately revealed than by Hosea.

> *"How can I give you up, Ephraim? How can I hand you over, Israel? How can I treat you like Admah? How can I make you like Zeboiim? My heart is changed within me; all my compassion is aroused. I will not carry out my fierce anger, nor will I turn and devastate Ephraim. For I am God, and not man— the Holy One among you. I will not come in wrath." (Hosea 11:8-9)*

Paul similarly taught that God's purpose in being slow to anger is to bring us to repentance (*Romans 2:4*), because his desire is that all men shall be saved (*1Timothy 2:4*).

Faithfulness.

The unanimous witness of all who have had dealings with

God is Love

God is that he keeps his word. He is utterly reliable, totally faithful, and he doesn't change his mind.

> *"God is not a man, that he should lie, nor a son of man, that he should change his mind. Does he speak and then not act? Does he promise and not fulfil?" (Numbers 23:19)*

> *"Your love, O Lord, reaches to the heavens, your faithfulness to the skies." (Psalm 36:5)*

> *"Your faithfulness continues through all generations; you established the earth, and it endures." (Psalm 119:90)*

> *"God, who has called you into fellowship with his Son Jesus Christ our Lord, is faithful." (1Corinthians 1:9)*

> *" if we are faithless, he will remain faithful, for he cannot disown himself." (2 Timothy 2:13)*

God's faithfulness is an expression of his mercy, his covenant love. Therefore, Jeremiah found this truth boiling up out of his troubled spirit:

> *Because of the Lord's great love (chesed) we are not consumed, for his compassions (râcham) never fail. They are new every morning; great is your faithfulness. (Lamentations 3:22-23)*

It is important to understand that God's faithfulness is to his word. He has bound himself to us by means of covenant promises. Out of his great mercy he took the initiative, announcing his intentions to men and women chosen for that purpose. He made a covenant with Abraham, who lived probably about 4000 years ago. One part of this promise to Abraham was that *"I will bless those who bless you and whoever curses you I will curse; and all peoples on earth will be blessed through you" (Genesis 12:3)*. Read on through the book of Genesis and you'll see how that promise began to operate. All true followers of Christ come within that covenant promise, which will continue to roll on until the end of time.

*I will not violate my covenant or alter what my
lips have uttered." (Psalm 89:34)
The Lord said to me, "You have seen correctly, for I am
watching to see that my word is fulfilled." (Jeremiah 1:12)*

In *Jeremiah 33:19-26* there is a wonderful passage in which God tells the prophet that his(God's) faithfulness to his word is as certain as the fact that night follows day. Thus, our security lies in the knowledge of God's faithfulness *("His faithfulness will be your shield and rampart." Psalm 91:4)*; and that brings peace of heart and mind.

*"Love and faithfulness meet together;
righteousness and peace kiss each other." (Psalm 85:10)*

Résumé.

Chapters 5 & 6 have given us an appreciation of God's nature that encourages us to draw near to him in confidence. Many say 'I'm not good enough to come into God's presence', or even 'I'm too far from him to come to church', not understanding that these are the very reasons why they need to do just that. What we have learned is that he will never reject even the most sin-sick, broken-hearted or timid person. Like the father in the story of the prodigal son, we are assured that the moment we turn our hearts to him, he rushes to greet us and take us with joy into his arms of love.

> This, this is the God we adore
> Our faithful, unchangeable Friend
> Whose love is as great as his power
> And neither knows measure nor end.
>
> 'Tis Jesus, the first and the last
> Whose Spirit shall guide us safe home
> We'll praise him for all that is past
> And trust him for all that's to come.
>
> Joseph Hart 1712-68

CHAPTER 7

Jesus Our High Priest

Christianity is Jewish.

In this Chapter we are concerned with those aspects of Jesus' priesthood which impact us as we seek God. Before we get into that, let us admit that the concept of Jesus as our High Priest is not widespread in the church. Is it important? After all, it may be argued that *Hebrews* was written by a Messianic Jew for Jewish Christians at a time when the church was overwhelmingly Jewish in membership and saw itself simply as the true expression of Judaism to which gentiles might be admitted on much the same basis as they were to Judaism itself. The church as a vast international gentile-led community with a microscopic Jewish component would have been unthinkable. Is the concept of Jesus as our High Priest one that resonates only with Messianic Jews? Is it needed by gentile Christians?

There is much confusion amongst Christians as to the relationship of the Church to Israel in God's economy. This is curious because Jesus taught clearly on this point:

> *"I have other sheep that are not of this sheep pen.*
> *I must bring them also. They too will listen to my voice,*
> *and there shall be one flock and one shepherd." (John 10:16)*

A probable cause of some of the confusion is what Paul says in *Romans 11:11*ff, as the metaphor is easily misunderstood. However, Paul's meaning is crystal clear in *Ephesians 2:11 - 3:6*, which is basically a restatement of Jesus' teaching.

Originally there were Jews and Gentiles, but the Gentiles could not benefit from the spiritual blessings of the Jewish covenants because the Torah acted as a 'wall' of separation. That 'wall' has now been demolished by Christ's death, with the result that nothing but unbelief now keeps Gentiles from receiving the full covenant blessings originally made available to Jews only. Jews and Gentiles now relate to God on the same basis (Here there is no Greek or Jew), and together form the Church, the body of Christ.

Thus, the Church has not replaced Israel in God's plans, nor has it been grafted onto Israel. It is a third and new entity, distinct from Israel and the Gentiles, which did not exist before Calvary. As Paul puts it: *His purpose was to create in himself one new man out of the two .... And in this one body to reconcile both of them to God through the cross (Ephesians 2:14-18).* With this understanding, we can now see what Paul meant in *Romans 11:11*ff.

In that parable, the olive tree represents the spiritual blessings available through and rooted in the Jewish covenants. Israel is represented by the natural branches, and indeed, the olive tree is owned by these natural branches. Nevertheless, the olive tree and the natural branches are two distinct entities. Gentiles are represented by the wild olive branches, and they have now been grafted into the root stock, the place of spiritual blessings. However, they are not grafted into Israel, since Israel is not the olive tree. Thus, both Jews and Gentiles partake of the covenant blessings on an equal basis, although a distinction remains between them in that the natural and wild branches remain as such. What matters, though, is *that through him we both have access to the Father by one Spirit (Ephesians 2:18).*

> *Consequently, you [Gentiles] are no longer foreigners and aliens, but fellow citizens with God's people and members of God's household (Ephesians 2:19).*

Therefore, we the church are heirs of all that was given by God to his chosen people, including the means by which we are to approach him, and our understanding of Jesus as our High Priest.

One of the problems in the early church as it exploded beyond the boundaries of Judaism was that some Jewish Christians were teaching that gentile Christians must keep the OT laws, especially those regarding food and special days such as the Sabbath. Paul, in particular, demolished such arguments, forcefully teaching about our freedom in Christ, and the fact that the church is a new and distinct entity. All that is now history, although modern analogies are to be found where New Age attitudes have infiltrated Christian thinking. However, the eternal truths embedded within the Pentateuch teaching on the tabernacle, and the wider issues of our approach to God, are in no way compromised and remain relevant for all people and all time.

Christ spent his time on earth as a Jew. Christianity was born out of Judaism and cradled in it. The Jewish scriptures (the OT) form more than three quarters of our Bible, including end-time prophecies of the highest concern to us because they are yet to be fulfilled. God's desire, shared with Moses, was for Israel to be a holy nation, a kingdom of priests, and that is precisely what will happen because God always gets his way. Therefore all gentile Christians are commanded by God to love and to pray for the Jews so that the Father will get his heart's desire.

The point of saying this is to establish the right mind-set as we approach God to worship him. It is in the context of worship and prayer that the essential Jewishness of Christianity is most evident in that the tabernacle teaching of both the Pentateuch and Hebrews is undeniably basic to a proper understanding of worship. The concept of priesthood reminds us of our responsibilities to both God and man, and the concept of the High Priestly office of Jesus reminds us of the way God responds to us as we seek his face.

Hebrews 9:4

The significance for Christians of the tabernacle symbolism is emphasised by inclusion of a summary description in *Hebrews*. The identity of the writer is not known but he was undoubtedly a Jew and most probably had been a Levitical priest (c.f. *Acts 6:7*). As such he himself may well have ministered in the Holy Place, though not of course in the Most Holy Place as he was not High Priest. His description of the tabernacle differs from that of *Exodus* because the veil of separation between the Holy Place and the Most Holy Place has now been torn open and it is the consequences of that act which he urgently presses upon us.

Sadly, in some English bibles the impact of his account is blunted by a mistranslation which appears to conflict with the description in *Exodus*. Thus (e.g.), the NIV rendering of *Hebrews 9:4* locates the 'golden altar of incense' in the Most Holy Place, whereas *Exodus* has it in the Holy Place. There is in fact no such conflict.

The issue turns on translation of the Greek word *thumiaterion*, of which *Hebrews 9:4* is the sole NT occurrence. It is given as 'altar of incense' in the NIV, but as 'censer' in the KJV. Other NT instances of the word 'altar' use a different Greek word, *thusiasterion*. There are two reasons for preferring the KJV here. (1) The Septuagint twice uses *thumiaterion* where the original Hebrew has 'censer'. (2) 'Censer' rather than 'altar' makes theological sense of the text. God's instructions for the Day of Atonement were clear:

> *The LORD said to Moses: "Tell your brother Aaron not to come whenever he chooses into the Most Holy Place behind the curtain in front of the atonement cover on the ark, or else he will die, because I appear in the cloud over the atonement cover."*

Jesus Our High Priest

> *"He is to take a censer full of burning coals from the altar before the LORD and two handfuls of finely ground fragrant incense and take them behind the curtain. He is to put the incense on the fire before the LORD, and the smoke of the incense will conceal the atonement cover above the Testimony, so that he will not die."*
> *(Leviticus 16:2,12-13)*

On this awesome annual occasion, the High Priest was to take his censer inside the Most Holy Place, using no less than *two handfuls of finely ground fragrant incense* to ensure that it emitted sufficient holy smoke to obscure the mercy seat where God appeared. This was his protection from death. On every other day of the year, a priest was to burn incense morning and evening at the golden altar but entirely within the Holy Place. Only on the Day of Atonement was the High Priest to perform this rite on the other side of the curtain.

Since Christ has entered the Most Holy Place with his own blood in a final, all-sufficient act of atonement, the dividing curtain is no longer needed, although the tabernacle paradigm remains of value to us. Therefore, when the writer of Hebrews saw into heaven, his attention was focussed upon the present reality and not upon the now-redundant twice-daily ceremonial at the golden altar located in the Holy Place.

The reality is that all Christians are priests of the Most High God with permanent access to his presence, there to worship and pray, thereby fulfilling what the annual burning of incense behind the curtain could only hint at. Thus, *Hebrews 9:4* tells us that the tabernacle model has not changed and remains relevant to us as Christians but that, crucially, the priestly ministry within it has altered. Moreover, as royal priests we minister within a legal framework but, in contrast to the Levitical priests, we are not constrained by it for it is the royal law of love. Indeed, it is love of God, to whom we owe everything, that draws us there in the first place.

With these concepts in place, we now focus on those aspects

of the High Priestly ministry of Jesus which impact us as we seek his face and meet with him.

Jesus our High Priest.

As High Priest, Jesus represents God to me and me to God (*Hebrews 5:1*). Moreover, being of the order of Melchisedek he does so on the basis of the power of an indestructible life (*Hebrews 7:16*).

> *There is one God and one mediator between God and men, the man Jesus Christ (1 Timothy 2:5)*

> *And whatever you do, whether in word or deed, do it all in the name of the Lord Jesus, giving thanks to God the Father through him (Colossians 3:17).*

Jesus represents God to us.

> *Jesus answered: .... "Anyone who has seen me has seen the Father" (John 14:6,9)*

> *No-one knows the Son except the Father, and no-one knows the Father except the Son and those to whom the Son chooses to reveal him. (Matthew 11:27)*

> *He [Christ] is the image of the invisible God. (Colossians 1:15 & 2 Corinthians 4:4))*

> *The Son is the radiance of God's glory and the exact representation of his being. (Hebrews 1:3)*

Jesus strengthens us for battle.

Melchisedek's encounter with Abraham was significantly timed. He met Abraham shortly after the latter had returned from a battle, specifically a battle for salvation of his relatives (Lot and his retinue) who had been abducted by an enemy. The lascivious rulers of the city (Sodom) from which Lot had been forcibly removed then confronted Abraham with a venal proposition which he rejected strenuously. Most significantly, however, Melchisedek intervened in this scenario, appearing to Abraham before the corrupt king of

Sodom could reach him.

Jesus, our High Priest after the order of Melchisedek, likewise strengthens us in the midst of the warfare into which new birth has pitched us, and he's always on schedule. As Christians we are familiar with the eucharistic emblems as a reminder of what Jesus has done for us, but Melchisedek's action in giving bread and wine to Abraham between battles implies divine empowering, and prefigures Jesus' teaching about himself in *John 6*.

The eucharist is far more than a memorial act. By it, in some mysterious but real way, we receive all the virtue of Jesus' flesh and blood, which becomes our strength for impending battles. Therefore, as we seek his face, it is appropriate to include celebration of the eucharist in the later stages of the time set apart for seeking God. It is, moreover, a meal of fellowship and mutual encouragement, as well as a divine encounter. The elders of Israel ate and drank on Sinai in God's presence (*Exodus 24:11*).

Jesus intercedes for us.
As my High Priest Jesus is the go-between who speaks to God on my behalf. The technical term for such a person is 'intercessor' from the Latin *inter* = between, and *cedere* = to go. This aspect of his ministry was foretold by *Isaiah (53:12)*:

"He bore the sin of many, and made intercession for the transgressors."

Several NT scriptures speak of Jesus as intercessor but there is confusion among commentators as to how these references are to be interpreted.

Our salvation comes in three parts: justification (completed at the moment of new birth), sanctification (the process of discipleship), and exaltation (to come). Hence the saying: 'I have been saved, I am being saved, and I shall be saved'. Jesus is actively involved in each phase. For this reason John saw in his vision (*Revelation 5:6*) a lamb standing in the centre of the throne, and therefore alive, whilst *looking as if it had been slain*, thereby representing simultaneously all three phases of his work to effect our complete salvation. We can see now how the intercession of Jesus fits into this framework. John specifically links Jesus' intercession for us to our continuing liability to sin.

> *"My dear children, I write this to you so that you will not sin. But if anybody does sin, we have one who speaks to the Father in our defence—Jesus Christ, the Righteous One. He is the atoning sacrifice for our sins, and not only for ours but also for the sins of the whole world."* (1 John 2:1-2)

It is claimed, rightly, that Jesus has already atoned for every sin at Calvary. Therefore, what need is there of such intercession on behalf of saints who sin? I believe that there are two aspects to it. (1) Although the work was completed at Calvary and applies for all eternity, there remains a present tense aspect. The blood of Christ is certainly available to cover our sins but those sins are nevertheless offensive to God. Therefore, in response to each sin repented of, Jesus speaks to the Father and removes the offence by covering it with his blood. (2) In respect of our sanctification, Jesus continually intercedes for us so that we shall grow up into the full spiritual stature that he has decreed for us individually, much as parents pray for their children. This will surely include prayers directed to helping us overcome our weaknesses.

Paul, too, says that Christ is also *interceding for us (Romans 8:34)*. This statement comes within a majestic passage in which he stresses that God is for us in every possible way and situation, and that as part of his total involvement with us in our humanity and in the fight of faith, Christ *is also interceding for us*.

A few verses previously Paul has described the way in which the Spirit intercedes for us (*Romans 8:26-27*). This intercession is linked to our weakness, specifically to our ignorance of what to pray, *but the Spirit intercedes for the saints in accordance with God's will*. Thus, both objective and subjective aspects of praying for us are covered. Christ prays to the Father about us and our needs, whilst the Spirit prays for us the prayers we want to pray for ourselves and others but cannot because of our ignorance. The writer of Hebrews covers the same issues as John and Paul in respect of Christ's intercession.

> *Therefore he is able to save completely those who come to God through him, because he always lives to intercede for them. (Hebrews 7:25)*

The word *completely* tells us that the intercession is on behalf of those who are already saved, as well as for those who have not yet come to the Father. A case in point is Jesus' prayer: *"Simon, Simon, Satan has asked to sift you as wheat. But I have prayed for you, Simon, that your faith may not fail" (Luke 22:31-32)*. Although this incident was before the cross, it still makes the point as it deals not with Simon's justification but with his development. It is the same for us. Jesus is committed to finish what he has begun in us *(Philippians 1:6)*.

For us, as for Simon, the key issue is that we train our minds and wills to choose God's ways and will in preference to our own, and in this we are assured that Jesus is backing us with his intercession at the right hand of the Father's throne. All of us are grateful to be assured of the prayers of others for us, because it shows that they care for us. How much more wonderful that Jesus himself intercedes for us in his office as eternal High Priest!

Likewise, the Holy Spirit is sent to be within us as the Comforter, the word meaning 'one who comes alongside to strengthen'. We see this in action in relation to Paul's statement that God *"will not let you be tempted beyond what you can bear. But when you are tempted, he will also provide a way out so that you can stand up under it" (1 Corinthians 10:13)*. In other words, God is actively limiting Satan's attacks upon us.

Thus, **as our High Priest**, Jesus has (1) atoned for our sins; (2) given the Holy Spirit to those who ask. (3) He limits Satan's attacks upon us and strengthens us to overcome them in future; (4) continually supports us in our fight of faith by his intercession. As Paul wrote: *"If God is for us, who can be against us?" (Romans 8:31)*.

Jesus is our brother.

As High Priest Jesus represents God to us but he does so as our brother. Because he is man as well as God, he is able to sympathise with us in our weaknesses. God created us in weakness (*Romans 6:19; 2Corinthians 13:4*): it is part of the human condition not altered at new birth. We are weak so that we shall look to God for our strength. Thus, we are to focus on these truths:

- that Jesus, our brother, while in the flesh and therefore sharing our human weaknesses nevertheless lived a sinless life and is thus *the pioneer and perfect example of faith (Hebrews 12:2)*[1.]

that whilst sympathising with us in our weaknesses, he nevertheless expects us to learn to walk in the victory he has won and made available to us.

Jesus, of all people, has the right to condemn us, but instead he's merciful because it's God's nature to have mercy. He has paid the price for our failures to overcome weaknesses, and therefore there is *no condemnation for those who are in Christ Jesus*. A classic example is Jesus' treatment of the woman caught in adultery (*John 8*). There is no hint of disapproval, judgement or condemnation, only the instruction not to do it again.

None of this should be taken to suggest tolerance of sin. The fact is that God has not only forgiven *us* and our sins, but has included our 'old man' with Christ on the cross, thereby dealing with the root cause of our sins. Thus, as Spirit-filled Christians we do not need to sin, although we do so because of failure to overcome weakness by his strength. As our brother in the flesh Jesus understands this perfectly. Indeed, it is surely one of the most awesome of all demonstrations of grace that he is able to *sympathise with our weaknesses*, despite the fact that he has already done for us all that is needed to enable us to live a sinless life.

What practical impact should these truths have upon us?
1. We are to come into our Father's presence with contrite and humble hearts, yet with confidence.
> *"Let us then approach the throne of grace with confidence, so that we may receive mercy and find grace to help us in our time of need." (Hebrews 4:16)*

Jesus Our High Priest

2. Appreciate that it is not a sin to be tempted. Jesus was tempted in every way just as we are, yet was without sin (*Hebrews 4:15*). Sin is yielding to temptation.

3. Accept that, like Jesus, we are to live in total dependence upon the Father, laying down our own agendas.

4. Refuse to accept condemnation because it is not of God. This does not mean that we are to reject constructive criticism or consider ourselves above it. Rather, living in humility before God and man we are to be confident that Christ, who of all people has the right to condemn us, never does so (*Romans 8:33-34*). Likewise, we are not to condemn others.

5. Put an end to false guilt. Real guilt must be dealt with by repentance, whereas false guilt crumbles in the face of God's truth about you. Whatever you confess to Christ is forgiven and covered by his blood: it is no more. Therefore *you may approach God with freedom and confidence (Ephesians 3:12)*. You are not a sinner doing your feeble best to serve God against all odds. You are a saint who sometimes sins. You are righteous and holy in God's sight because the Righteous One lives in you. You are able to do all things through him, and to live in the good of Christ's victory! Live by these truths and you will be free from false guilt.

> 1.
> With joy we meditate the grace
> Of our High Priest above
> His heart is made of tenderness
> And ever yearns with love.
>
> 2.
> Touched with a sympathy within
> He knows our feeble frame
> He knows what sore temptations mean
> For he hath felt the same.

3.
He in the days of feeble flesh
Poured out his cries and tears
And, though exalted, feels afresh
What every member bears.

4.
He'll never quench the smoking flax
But raise it to a flame
The bruisèd reed he never breaks
Nor scorns the meanest name.

5.
Then let our humble faith address
His mercy and his power
We shall obtain delivering grace
In the distressing hour.

Isaac Watts (1674-1748)

Chapter 8

Ministry To God

Royal Priesthood.

The priests of Israel were born into the tribe of Levi, consecrated for service to God, anointed with holy oil, and performed prescribed duties which included offering ritual sacrifices to God. They wore ceremonial dress made of fine linen, but were forbidden to wear woolen garments lest they sweated in them.

As royal priests, we have been born into a priestly kingdom, are consecrated to God, have his Spirit resident within and his anointing upon us. As we walk in obedience to Jesus we are seen to be clothed in his righteousness and free from self-generated effort. Theirs was the 'shadow', ours the reality. Moreover, our priesthood, like that of Jesus, is after the order of Melchisedek because we minister in the power of the endless life of the indwelling Holy Spirit. Therefore, our ministry, both to God and to man, far exceeds that of Israel's priests in scope, power and cost. As with Jesus, our priesthood is to be characterised by obedience to the Father, and self-sacrifice.

Ministry to God.
He whose walk is blameless will minister to me. (Psalm 101:6)

God's desire is for a kingdom of priests. Thus, we exist to know and minister to our God. This is the first call upon our lives, hearts, time and energy: to worship and minister to God. Any other order is out of order. This is the priestly calling and function of every Christian,

Self-sacrifice. The God-ward function of the Levitical priesthood as it developed during Israel's history was to offer sacrifices and sing praises *(1 Chronicles 6:31-32; 2 Chronicles 20:18-21)*. Our sacrifices are more costly than theirs since the cost is to the flesh, not the pocket. We are living sacrifices who must daily reaffirm the death with Christ of our *old man*.

> *The LORD said to Moses: "Give Aaron and his sons this*
> *command: 'These are the regulations for the burnt*
> *offering: The burnt offering is to remain on the altar hearth*
> *throughout the night, till morning, and the fire must be*
> *kept burning on the altar. ...... The fire must be kept burning*
> *on the altar continuously; it must not go out." (Leviticus 6:8-13)*

> *Then he said to them all: "If anyone would come after me,*
> *he must deny himself and take up his cross daily*
> *and follow me." (Luke 9:23)*

> *"I tell you the truth, unless a kernel of wheat falls to*
> *the ground and dies, it remains only a single seed. But if it dies,*
> *it produces many seeds. The man who loves his life will lose it,*
> *while the man who hates his life in this world will keep it*
> *for eternal life." (John 12:24-25)*

> *"I die every day." (1 Corinthians 15:31)*

> "Those who belong to Christ Jesus have crucified the
> sinful nature with its passions and desires." *(Galatians 5:24)*

The fire on the altar [of my heart] must be kept burning, my zeal, passion, devotion and love must not grow cold. This is no ceremonial exercise but outward proof that in my innermost being I have willingly embraced the full meaning of the priesthood in the power of the endless life that is mine in Christ. Glory to God! This self-sacrifice releases me for Spirit-led service both to God and man.

Worship.

Jesus' teaching on worship was brief and to the point. God is Spirit. Therefore he must be worshipped in the spirit, not in the flesh. Moreover, the Holy Spirit is the Spirit of Truth, meaning that his directions will always conform to scripture, which he inspired in the first place. Thus:

> "A time is coming and has now come when the true
> worshipers will worship the Father in spirit and truth, for
> they are the kind of worshipers the Father seeks.
> God is spirit, and his worshipers must worship
> in spirit and in truth." *(John 4:23-24)*

> "Your worship must engage your spirit in the pursuit of
> truth. That's the kind of people the Father is looking out for:
> those who are simply and honestly themselves before him
> in their worship. God is sheer being itself - Spirit.
> Those who worship him must do it out of their very being,
> their spirits, their true selves, in adoration."
> *(John 4:23-24 The Message)*

God deals with us on a need-to-know basis. He reveals what we need to know, and no more, so that we shall relate to him by faith. Jesus' teaching on worship is all that we need to know in order to worship the Father acceptably. Its brevity and simplicity contrasts dramatically with the frenetic activity of today's worship industry. Even among Pentecostal and Charismatic churches Spirit-led worship is rare. The devil, who may well have been heaven's worship leader before his downfall, craves worship *(Luke 4:5-8)*. He may not receive it from Christians but he is undoubtedly incredibly successful in restricting our worship of God by a spirit of control and through man-made traditions.

It is in the conduct of worship that all that we have now reviewed about the tabernacle and its associated priestly ministry finds its most direct application. God's desire is that we proceed in our worship from the outer court, through the Holy Place, and into the Most Holy Place, there to meet with him. It is there, in one-to-one communion with God, as his Spirit touches your spirit, that worship pours like rivers from your heart. There, where it feels sometimes as though every cell in your body, every fibre of your being is crying out in joyful recognition of your Lord, you know beyond a shadow of doubt that this is why you were created. Not fully conscious of what is happening around you, probably with tears of joy, you are caught up into the worship of heaven. It is the place of hearing God, where prophecy is birthed, vision imparted, and intercession conceived. You are "Lost in wonder, love and praise". This is the worship our Father wants from his children.

How do we get there? By faith, of course, and most evidently by obeying the Spirit's leading. That said, we also need a platform of truth, the biblical teaching on how God is to be approached, to light our path (*Psalm 119:105*), much of which we have covered in preceding chapters.

The first court.

The first court of the tabernacle was in the open air, visible to all. Entrance is through the gateway of thanksgiving into the courtyard of praise. Not only is this a biblical command, it establishes the right heart attitude for worship. We do not come to be 'topped up' for the week ahead, but to worship God. Yes, of course he responds with blessings, and we are to come expecting to receive, but our hearts are to be focussed on ministering to him.

This is the part of the service when we encourage each other ("Come on and celebrate") and ourselves ("Praise, my soul, the King of Heaven"). Praise blesses God, screws up the devil, and lifts us out of ourselves. It is good medicine. Therefore, be free, exuberant, and wholehearted in your praise of God. Dance, wave flags and banners. Make Palm Sunday look like a side show! The Holy One of God is among you.

Here also is the place to confess sin and receive forgiveness on the basis of Jesus' sacrifice of his own life. The bronze altar and the washing bowl remind us that we must be cleansed before drawing closer to him. Pastors know well that people come into church in all sorts and conditions. The spiritually mature, elders/leaders, the music group will (or should) be able to 'carry' the worship at this stage while the Pastor (and/or others) assure the penitent that they are forgiven. Christ gave his church authority, not to forgive sins, but to pronounce that God has forgiven all that has been confessed (*John 20:23*). Some may come into your service under such a burden of sin and misery that the rest of the service will be meaningless to them without absolution. If the Spirit so directs, a limited amount of personal ministry may be appropriate at this stage whilst the service continues around you. Those in pain cannot focus on worship, so heal them.

Silence in worship.
When the Holy Spirit makes his presence felt during worship there is often an involuntary silence or stillness. The worship leader or music group leader tends to be uneasy at such times: he doesn't know what to do and therefore feels threatened or exposed - so he makes a move of his own.

The answer to such silences, as in any other situation in which you don't know what God is saying, is to do nothing until you hear from him, however long that takes. I have waited as long as 30 minutes in such circumstances, and they are very precious times. With a congregation not used to stillness you will need to explain what is happening, and encourage them to open their hearts to God as he reveals himself.

Some find extended silence threatening. Their lives are so full of busyness, chatter, and background noise that they are frightened to be trapped alone with self. But our Father wants our full and undivided attention, and he can get it best through silence. It is all too easy to 'hide' in worship, to go through the externals of it along with others, but to shelter from God. In the silence it's you and him, and you have a choice. Sit it out, twiddle your thumbs, occupy your mind with your own thoughts, or allow the Spirit free access to your heart. If you really did come to the service to meet with God, you'll embrace these silences as the high point of your day. How many say: "I wish I heard God like you do"? Well, they can!

The second and third courts.

The Spirit will show those leading when it is time to move on from praise to worship. The difference between praise and worship is this: we praise God for what he has done, we worship him for what he is. The transition does not have to be with 'worshipful' songs. You may sing in tongues, use silence, or just enjoy God individually as the musicians maintain a flow of sound under the Spirit's direction.

The second and third courts are the two compartments of the tent of the tabernacle. The curtain of separation is now torn apart and the ministry of the one flows into the other, as is shown by *Hebrews 9:4* (c.f. Chapter 7). Nevertheless, a valuable distinction between the two areas remains.

The light in the Holy Place is that of the seven-branched candlestick, the menorah, meaning that here the Spirit directs all that happens. It is the place of worship in tongues, of ministry using the gifts of the Spirit, of fellowship around the word of God - preaching and teaching. Many churches are content to remain there. It has become familiar. It is gentle, warm, comforting, and leaders are happy to be seen to minister to the people in the power of the Spirit.

Church, know that this is but the ante-chamber to the Most Holy Place where God wants you to fellowship with him face to face. "Good is the enemy of the best" and nowhere more so than in the second court of the tabernacle.

Here, in the secret place of the Most High God, it is you and him, one to one. It is a place of silence and peace, of total reality and transparency. Worship pours out of you as you are lifted into his presence and the Spirit within you cries out in joy, *Abba, Father!* As a bride and her new husband look adoringly into each others' eyes, so you are lost in God. Time loses its meaning because you are in eternity.

In this Most Holy Place you are concerned more with the fruit of the Spirit than with his gifts. That you are there at all is proof that you are totally acceptable to him, that he sees you as righteous and holy because of the life of Christ within you. You need never again doubt your salvation. You are a saint, a holy one, created to walk this earth as a miniature colony of the kingdom of God, to make Jesus known. People will want to know you because of the light within you, whilst being restrained by the anointing upon you.

Leading worship.
The tabernacle model defines the general framework of our approach to God but it must not be used slavishly or it too will become to us a tradition. Above all, it tells us that there is a place of intimate meeting with God accessible to all who will enter in. This is always true for each of us individually, but for a whole congregation to enter that place, the worship must be led by those who understand how to meet with God, and how to submit to the leading of the Holy Spirit.

One thing must be clearly understood. Spirit-led worship will never be established in a church unless the Pastor is wholeheartedly devoted to it. He himself may or may not be the worship leader, but he must be seen to lead the congregation in pressing into the presence of God, even if others have been deputed to lead it up front.

In Charismatic and Pentecostal churches worship is often led by the music group, the Pastor being in overall charge of the meeting but standing aside during the time allocated to singing. The danger of that is that the singing part of the meeting can become decoupled from the rest, and may only be an item within a set and traditional order of service. The whole meeting must be submitted to the Spirit's leading, even to the extent of being willing to abandon prepared items, including the sermon.

Two distinct functions.
In Spirit-led worship it is important to distinguish between worship leader (WL) and music group leader (MGL). Musicians have a demanding technical job to do, the more so if they are not of professional standard, as few are. It is essential for the musicians, especially the MGL, to hear God for themselves in respect of the musical direction of the meeting, but the WL must listen to the Spirit for the overall direction of the meeting. The WL need not be a musician and, commonly, will be the Pastor. There are exceptions to this scheme, but they are few and far between. A MGL who is nationally or internationally prominent may even become a barrier to spiritual progress in the worship, because eyes are on him rather than the Lord.

Preparing to lead worship.
In spiritual things you can lead only where you have been yourself. The worship leader must, therefore, know the way into the Most Holy Place if he/she is to lead the people there. This is not just intellectual knowledge, but a heart issue. Moreover, it is not a question of having been there occasionally. To lead worship you must come *from* the Most Holy Place, to gather the people and take them back there with you. It is a spiritual nonsense to expect to lead others in worship if you yourself have not recently come from meeting with Christ.

The anointing oil must be freshly upon you. Yesterday's anointing was for yesterday. The Israelis were told by God to gather manna daily because it would not keep overnight (*Exodus 16:19-20*). The fire on the altar of sacrifice must never go out, a spiritual instruction of such urgency that it is repeated three times in a brief passage (*Leviticus 6:8-13*). And Christ instructs his followers to take up their cross daily. In such ways God impresses upon us his expectation of at least daily meaningful fellowship with us. It is not a matter of regulations and timetables. Love is the driving force. There is to be about it that longing and excitement, that tingling joy, of looking for, meeting with and revelling in the presence of the One you love above all others. The Song of Songs reflects this perfectly. Thus, it is not so much the service or meeting which needs to be prepared, but those who will lead it.

Spirit-led worship.

The job of the **Worship Leader** (WL) is to listen to the Holy Spirit and do what he says. All who belong to Christ hear his voice (*John 8:48;10:4*), although some become more practised than others. The WL must know how to hear God. God speaks Spirit to spirit and it is in your spirit that you will hear/sense/feel what he is saying. How? By faith. As you gain experience leading worship your faith in that ability will grow. One of the glories of Spirit-led worship is that it's never the same twice over. The Holy Spirit keeps it fresh, and that is one of the signs that you really are following his leading. But don't seek variety for its own sake - that too may become a tradition to you. There are 'seasons' in the things of the Spirit, and he may keep you in a particular form of worship for weeks at a time before he moves you into a different 'stream' of the river of his purposes (*Psalm 46:4*).

The music group.

The primary qualification for playing or singing in the music group/choir is not musicianship but that you are a worshipper. Our practice is that no-one is allowed into the music group until they have been six months as a worshipper in the congregation, even if they are a professional musician. They must first get their heart so fixed upon worshipping Christ that they will no longer be tempted to perform. The frustration of not being used, especially when your talents and training exceed those up front, is part of the process of getting your heart right with God. Self wants to perform, but God is looking for a heart so set upon worshipping him that the privilege of being with him in the Most Holy Place becomes your joy and satisfaction. Then he can safely allow you to join the music group because you will be playing to him under the Spirit's direction, for his satisfaction, not performing for the people.

It is not the function of **the music group leader** (MGL) to choose what to play/sing. That is for the Spirit to direct. The MGL himself/herself may well hear what God wants him to play, and that's fine, but he should not turn up with a list of songs to be used in the meeting: that would be to take direction of the worship from the Spirit. Indeed, it may be one of those occasions on which the Lord does not want songs to be used, only singing in the Spirit.

The MGL is subject to the leading of the WL at all times. Moreover, with few exceptions, the MGL should not address the meeting, and certainly not talk between songs or in any other way take the focus off God. He needs all his attention for hearing God, communicating with the others in his group, and dealing with musical technicalities. The WL is the one who communicates with the congregation.

In practice.

You are to lead worship tomorrow morning. It is a responsibility as well as a privilege and joy. Today you will be sure to spend time alone with God. He may show you how he wants the meeting to go, or something specific to include. Or he may not. You fall asleep worshipping and therefore wake up doing the same. Again, you will spend time with God before going out, although if you are the mother of three small children all under school age he'll understand if you cannot! Hopefully, you will have time to pray with other leaders and the music group, not so much to put your requests to God as to submit to him and hear his directions. Let those present share what they are hearing. This is your general direction for the meeting, although its outworking may surprise you.

Dear Pastor.

To lead worship in this way may require a major shift of thinking and practice. Pastors like to be in control - and that's the problem! If they have not planned the meeting they feel insecure. To step out in front of a few tens, hundreds or even thousands to lead worship with nothing but yourself prepared is exciting. You have nothing lined up, therefore you know that the Spirit will turn up and that it will be glorious! Your confidence is in God alone, which is where he wants it. Pastor - try it!

In leading worship I live by *Psalm 81:10. "I am the LORD your God. ... Open wide your mouth and I will fill it."* On hundreds of occasions I have walked out in front of a congregation with this verse in mind, nothing prepared, but with a tingling sense of excitement and expectation that God is about to move. He always does! I may begin by welcoming people to the meeting. I may simply chat about whatever comes into my head: something I have recently understood from my Bible study, my wife's new dress, a piece of church news, a joke, something one of our grandchildren did - anything, but I am listening for that special moment when the Spirit will drop in something beautiful that will take us right into the Father's presence.

Equally, I may stand before the people in silence, eyes closed, worshipping in my spirit. Minutes pass, the anointing comes down like a blanket, people are meeting with God, there are tears of joy, some are already on their faces. Still not a word has been spoken, no music played, but you have led the people into the Most Holy Place. Pastor, WL, you have an anointing from the Holy One. That anointing increases as you fellowship with the Holy Spirit. Have confidence, therefore, to stand before your people and simply release the anointing to them. It doesn't take five bouncy songs, three worshipful ones, and then 20 seconds of singing in tongues to enter the Most Holy Place. You can start there.

Above all, keep the focus on God. Don't let concentration slip, and make sure that your MGL doesn't talk to the people between songs. A congregation who are practised in worship in the Spirit can continue for a couple of hours or more without a break

Worship and sacrifice.
The association of worship with sacrifice is undeniable. By the tabernacle model God shows that intimacy with him is approached by way of the bronze altar of sacrifice and the washing bowl. It is commonly assumed, especially in charismatic circles, that the NT church equivalent is 'the sacrifice of praise' (*Jeremiah 33:11KJV; Hebrews 13:15*) but this needs qualification. The lively performance of hymns and songs of praise is not necessarily to be equated with cost, and praise which costs nothing is worth just that.

In NT terms 'sacrifice' means dealing with the flesh, and it is always costly. We are called to be 'living sacrifices' (*Romans 12:1*), that is, to continually say 'no' to every subtle manifestation of our 'old man' which has been nailed to Christ's cross (*Titus 2:12*).

God's intention is that we live permanently in that depth of intimate relationship with him of which the Most Holy Place is a representation. In practice, getting there is often a process, sometimes a lengthy one. It is as if, like the High Priests of Israel, we pay repeated visits to the Most Holy Place. In his grace he blesses us at each stage of this developing intimacy, but by that same grace he plants in our hearts the desire to go deeper. Each step requires progressive sacrifice until *'the fear of the Lord'* so grips our hearts that we are prepared to be purged of all that is not of him, so that we may live permanently in his presence. Then, indeed, the praise and worship which pour from our hearts as we see the Lamb upon his throne may truly be called 'the sacrifice of praise'.

God requires that worship take pride of place in our hearts. The plagues of Egypt were released precisely because Pharaoh refused God's demand to let my people go, so that they may worship me. The book of Revelation shows plainly that judgement is inevitable upon anyone or any system that interferes with the worship of God.

> "The greatest evil that we face from the outside
> world is the prevention of our worship of God.
> The greatest evil we face inside the church is
> the subversion of our worship." (Selwyn Hughes)

You have an open heaven.

Church, know that you have an open heaven. It was opened the moment Jesus died on the cross, as indicated by the torn curtain in the Jerusalem temple. Nothing, no-one, not even the devil in person, can close that open access. Oh yes, there may be 'darkness' over your city or town, and it may sometimes come upon you as you begin your meeting but, like a cloud, you know that the sun is shining above it. You have God-given authority to demolish that darkness. As you begin to do so, God backs you with his supernatural power and the darkness is rolled back.

Rejoice when you are faced with such opposition. God has allowed it to train you in overcoming the Evil One and you are about to take fresh spiritual territory. Declare the name of Jesus, shout (yes, shout!) his praises, exalt him exuberantly, dance before him with joy, prophesy on the musical instruments, revel in the victory that is yours in Christ. God inhabits the praises of his people, and where God is present the devil will not be. Hallelujah! Never allow demonic opposition to restrain your worship of God.

Chapter 9

How To Seek The Lord

Seeking the Lord takes time.
It cannot be hurried because God cannot be hurried. Whilst our daily time with the word and in prayer includes, hopefully, some aspects of seeking his face, waiting upon him, loving him for himself alone, it remains true that we do need to set aside occasions when we may spend more extended time with him. Therefore, along with the many scriptural injunctions to seek God, are many more which tell us to 'wait' upon or to 'watch' for him. After all, he is the King of kings and it is only right that we should be ready and willing to wait upon him, however long that may take. He has his own agenda for the heart and it may take quite some time to tune into that.

*"In the morning, O LORD, you hear my voice; in the morning
I lay my requests before you and wait in expectation." (Psalm 5:3)*

*"Wait for the LORD; be strong and take heart and
wait for the LORD." (Psalm 27:14)*

*"We wait in hope for the LORD; he is our help and our shield."
(Psalm 33:20)*

*"Be still before the LORD and wait patiently for him."
(Psalm 37:7)*

"Wait for the LORD and keep his way." (Psalm 37:34)

*"I wait for you, O LORD; you will answer,
O Lord my God." (Psalm 38:15)*

*"I waited patiently for the LORD; he turned to me
and heard my cry." (Psalm 40:1)*

"Be still and know that I am God." (Psalm 46:10)

*"O my Strength, I watch for you: you O God are my fortress."
(Psalm 59:9)*

*"I wait for the LORD, my soul waits, and in his word
I put my hope. My soul waits for the Lord more than
watchmen wait for the morning." (Psalm 130:5-6)*

*"Yes, LORD, walking in the way of your laws,
we wait for you; your name and renown are the
desire of our hearts." (Isaiah 26:8)*

*"Yet the LORD longs to be gracious to you;
he rises to show you compassion. For the LORD is a God
of justice. Blessed are all who wait for him!" (Isaiah 30:18)*

"Since ancient times no one has heard, no ear has perceived,

*no eye has seen any God besides you, who acts on behalf of
those who wait for him." (Isaiah 64:4)*

*I say to myself, "The LORD is my portion; therefore I
will wait for him." It is good to wait quietly for the salvation
of the LORD. (Lamentations 3:24,26)*

*"But you must return to your God; maintain love and justice,
and wait for your God always." (Hosea 12:6)*

*"But as for me, I watch in hope for the LORD, I wait for God
my Saviour; my God will hear me." (Micah 7:7)*

"Therefore wait for me," declares the LORD. (Zephaniah 3:8)

*"Watch and pray so that you will not fall into temptation."
(Mark 14:38)*

*On one occasion, while he was eating with them,
he gave them this command: "Do not leave Jerusalem,
but wait for the gift my Father promised, which you have
heard me speak about." (Acts 1:4)*

Thus, there is an inescapable connection between seeking God and waiting. It is not that he is reluctant to answer, but that he would have our whole attention focussed upon himself. Most of us live lives filled with the legitimate demands of family, friends, work and church, not to mention personal interests, and the torrent of media output thrown daily across our paths. In this latter aspect, there is surely a demonic influence, since the result is the opposite of entering into the 'rest' God has prepared for those who seek him. For these reasons alone, time is needed to still our hearts in his presence.

Then I understood.
There are deeper causes of unrest: heart issues, old hurts, hidden agendas, loom out of the mist and fog of our emotions as we rest in his presence.

There is more. Wait in his presence with a stilled heart and, like the writer of *Psalm 73*, you will discover answers to your deepest concerns. They may not be the answers you expect, and commonly will not be direct answers at all, but by them God will change your heart and therefore also your thinking.

> *"For my thoughts are not your thoughts, neither are your ways my ways," declares the LORD. "As the heavens are higher than the earth, so are my ways higher than your ways and my thoughts than your thoughts."*
> *(Isaiah 55:8-9)*

> *"But as for me, my feet had almost slipped; I had nearly lost my foothold. For I envied the arrogant when I saw the prosperity of the wicked. Surely in vain have I kept my heart pure; in vain have I washed my hands in innocence. When I tried to understand all this, it was oppressive to me till I entered the sanctuary of God; then I understood their final destiny." (Psalm 73:2-3, 13, 16-17)*

> *."... you must wait seven days until I come to you and tell you what you are to do."(1 Samuel 10:8)*

> *Ten days later the word of the LORD came to Jeremiah. (Jeremiah 42:7)*

> *"I will stand at my watch and station myself on the ramparts: I will look to see what he will say to me .... For the revelation awaits an appointed time; it speaks of the end and will not prove false. Though it linger, wait for it; it will certainly come and will not delay." (Habakuk 2:1,3)*

Thereby, we begin to understand why there is no substitute for spending extended time in quietness before God. It is something that the soul of modern man finds hard. The will is king of the soul, but it must abdicate in favour of the Spirit. Mind and will must no longer dominate our lives. We are to learn what it means to enter his rest (*Hebrews 4:5*), to cease from striving. He is the One who must set the agenda as we seek his face. The timing, content and manner of it are to be his.

> *"As the eyes of slaves look to the hand of their master,*
> *as the eyes of a maid look to the hand of her mistress,*
> *so our eyes look to the LORD our God, till he shows*
> *us his mercy." (Psalm 123:2)*

Righteousness and seeking God.

Righteousness and justice are the foundation of his throne (*Psalm 89:14;97:2*). Since the whole aim of seeking God is to enter the Most Holy Place, the place of his presence, it follows that there must be a link with righteousness. Indeed, the very structure of Moses' tabernacle and its' prescribed rituals make clear beyond doubt that only cleansed and consecrated priests may enter the inner courts. God is holy and no unrighteous thing may enter his presence. Therefore, for those who seek the Lord, as for the ancient priests of Israel, his presence is entered by way of the bronze altar of sacrifice and the bronze washing bowl, now given reality in the blood of Christ and a righteous lifestyle made possible by the indwelling Holy Spirit (*Hebrews 10:19-22*). Christ is our righteousness. therefore, he says, I am the way to the Father. Since we are in him, and he in us, we are able to enter the Father's presence.

The scriptures repeatedly stress the connection between righteousness and drawing close to God. Thus:

> *"Anyone who lives on milk, being still an infant, is not*
> *acquainted with the teaching about righteousness."*
> *(Hebrews 5:13)*

> *In the eighth year of his reign, while he [King Josiah] was*
> *still young, he began to seek the God of his father David.*
> *In his twelfth year he began to purge Judah and Jerusalem*
> *of high places, Asherah poles, carved idols and cast images.*
> *(2 Chronicles 34:3)*

> *So the Israelites who had returned from the exile ate it*
> *[the Passover], together with all who had separated*
> *themselves from the unclean practices of their Gentile*
> *neighbours in order to seek the LORD, the God of Israel.*

(Ezra 6:21)

"Evil men do not understand justice, but those who seek the LORD understand it fully." (Proverbs 28:5)

"Listen to me, you who pursue righteousness and who seek the LORD: Look to the rock from which you were cut and to the quarry from which you were hewn." (Isaiah 51:1)

"Sow for yourselves righteousness, reap the fruit of unfailing love, and break up your unploughed ground; for it is time to seek the LORD, until he comes and showers righteousness on you." (Hosea 10:12)

"Seek the LORD, all you humble of the land, you who do what he commands. Seek righteousness, seek humility; perhaps you will be sheltered on the day of the Lord's anger." (Zephaniah 2:3)

"But seek first his kingdom and his righteousness, and all these things will be given to you as well." (Matthew 6:33)

Thus, as we seek his face, time must be given to allow the Holy Spirit to search our hearts and to put his spotlight on whatever he chooses.

Who am I?

The words we studied in Chapters 5 & 6 prepare us for meeting with God in that they tell us something of what he is like, and how he will receive us. This should give us great confidence as we seek him. The other side of the coin is that we need to know how he sees us

1. **The spiritual fact of who you are in Christ.** When you came to Christ you were 'justified'. That is, your sins were forgiven, you yourself were forgiven, you were put into a right relationship with God, and the Holy Spirit came to live in you. Therefore scripture

says that you are a 'saint' (the word means 'holy one'), and no longer a 'sinner'.

You are a *new creation (2 Corinthians 5:17)*, something that didn't exist before, because your new identity is your new Spirit-filled life in Christ, and the fact that you are now, first and foremost, a citizen of heaven. Christ within you is your righteousness. That's why Paul *(Romans 1:17)* talks about *"a righteousness from God .... a righteousness that is by faith from first to last"*. This work of justification was done the instant you gave your life to Christ. It was all God's work, it is complete and perfect, and it is the basis of your confidence in approaching the throne of grace.

> He receives you as he receives his beloved Son,
> because of the life of his Son within you.

2. **You are a son.** Thus, Paul:

   "You are all sons of God through faith in Christ Jesus, for all of you who were baptised into Christ have clothed yourselves with Christ." (Galatians 3:26-27)

   But when the time had fully come, God sent his Son, born of a woman, born under law, to redeem those under law, that we might receive the full rights of sons. Because you are sons, God sent the Spirit of his Son into our hearts, the Spirit who calls out, "Abba, Father." So you are no longer a slave, but a son; and since you are a son, God has made you also an heir. (Galatians 4:4-7)

   In scripture 'son' is a unisex term. *"There is neither Jew nor Greek, slave nor free, male nor female, for you are all one in Christ Jesus"* *(Galatians 3:28)*. Sons are precious to their father, they live with him and have free access to him. More, they are loved by him as part of his very self, and they will inherit what is his. This may not have been your experience of fatherhood on earth, but the scriptures talk of our heavenly Father who *is* perfect in all his ways.

   Know then, that as you seek his face you are not a poor beggar seeking favours. You have all the rights of a son of God. He knows everything about you, your unspoken thoughts, fears, desires, fantasies, and the things of which you are ashamed, yet he responds with delight as you approach him. You are family, you are his, and he'll never give up on you. Therefore, come to him confidently.

> *"For we do not have a high priest who is unable to sympathise with our weaknesses, but we have one who has been tempted in every way, just as we are—yet was without sin. Let us then approach the throne of grace with confidence, so that we may receive mercy and find grace to help us in our time of need." (Hebrews 4:15-16)*

CHAPTER 10

In Practice

Relationships are the key indicator.
Relationships are central to God's kingdom. As the Bible opens we glimpse God and man in unclouded face-to-face relationship. Moreover, the man and his mate are there together precisely because God is concerned that the man shall have a partner with whom he can share his life.

> *The LORD God said, "It is not good for the man to be alone. I will make a helper suitable for him." Genesis 2:18)*

Later, Moses would generalise these truths, and Jesus would affirm them: we are to love God first, and our neighbour as ourself.

In Practice

> *Hear, O Israel: The Lord our God, the Lord is one. Love the
> Lord your God with all your heart and with all your soul
> and with all your strength. (Deuteronomy 6:4-5)*

> *"Do not seek revenge or bear a grudge against one of
> your people, but love your neighbor as yourself.
> I am the LORD." (Leviticus 19:18)*

> *One of the teachers of the law came and heard them
> debating. Noticing that Jesus had given them a good
> answer, he asked him, "Of all the commandments,
> which is the most important?" "The most important one,"
> answered Jesus, "is this: 'Hear, O Israel, the Lord our God,
> the Lord is one. Love the Lord your God with all
> your heart and with all your soul and with all your mind
> and with all your strength.' The second is this:
> 'Love your neighbor as yourself.' There is no commandment
> greater than these." (Mark 12:28-31)*

Thus, there is a corporate aspect to seeking God's face. Our individual relationship with him is vital but, at the end of the day, the aim is a church-bride prepared for Christ. Indeed, the two aspects are linked, as the first letter of John teaches so eloquently: 1 John 4:7-21 especially.

In practice, this means that in a church or group that sets out to seek God's face consistently, personal relationships will also deepen. You know what it's like when you come upon two lovers unexpectedly: for a brief moment, as they turn to you in surprise, the radiance of the love they have been showing to each other is turned also upon you! It's like that when you've been meeting with God. The proof that people have met with God is in the deepening of their relationships.

Practical matters.
> *"Take words with you and return to the Lord." (Hosea 14:2)*

Seeking the Lord takes time. If you can give only an evening to it you'll be blessed. In a day much more can be done, and a week is yet more productive. What follows is an outline of one way in which I have led groups into God's presence, given a whole day.

There is no formula for seeking the Lord because it is a matter of following the leading of the Holy Spirit. Moreover, the circumstances and causes of seeking his face will differ. Nevertheless, the general principles of our approach to God as specified in scripture apply. Above all, follow the Holy Spirit's direction. Our intention is to enter the Most Holy Place, and the only possible guide is the Holy Spirit.

The content of what needs to be given by way of spiritual direction depends upon the maturity of those present. In general, it is wise to assume rather little, unless one is with people one knows well. For example, not uncommonly a time of seeking God reveals people who find that they have no real personal relationship with him at all: they may not even be saved. Therefore, it is unwise to try to go deep too quickly. Lay the foundations carefully and unhurriedly.

As you seek God, you have his promise that you *will* 'find' him. He will respond to your approach because he is faithful to his word. However, do not be surprised if the early stages, especially, seem unproductive and more like hard work. Waiting upon him means just that. It takes time for tensions arising from a pressured lifestyle to subside, and for the heart to be still before your Creator. Encourage people to persevere and not to drop out during the time set aside for seeking God.

"Weeping may remain for a night, but rejoicing comes in the morning." (Psalm 30:5)

Depending upon the spiritual maturity of those present, it may be possible to have hours of uninterrupted personal time with the Lord. In other circumstances, it may be necessary to leave folk no more than 15 or 20 minutes without further help.

1. Start by allaying fears. Some will come expectant and well

In Practice

prepared, others will probably be apprehensive, especially if they have not done this sort of thing before. So lighten the atmosphere, break the ice, let the joy and peace of the Lord flow out of you. Get folk to introduce themselves to each other, perhaps share a hug or two. You're here to enjoy God, not to take medicine! Yes, he'll probably face us with a few things we need to sort out, but he'll do it with compassion and entirely without condemnation.

Encourage people to have faith for meeting with God, by using scriptures such as:

> *Seek the LORD while he may be found; call on him while he is near. Let the wicked forsake his way and the evil man his thoughts. Let him turn to the LORD, and he will have mercy on him, and to our God, for he will freely pardon. (Isaiah 55:6-7)*

> *Let us acknowledge the LORD; let us press on to acknowledge him. As surely as the sun rises, he will appear; he will come to us like the winter rains, like the spring rains that water the earth." (Hosea 6:3)*

Remind people that God *has not given us a spirit of fear, but of power and love and of a sound mind (2 Timothy 1:7NKJV)*. As we submit ourselves to God, we always remain in control: he will never overrule our freewill. *The spirits of prophets are subject to the control of prophets (1 Corinthians 14:32)*, and we are all heirs of the prophets (*Acts 3:25*).

2. Get into thanksgiving, praise and worship. In this, as in everything, submit fully to the direction of the Spirit. Expect to enter the Most Holy Place, to meet with God as you worship. Worship in tongues as well as in your own language. Allow time for everyone to worship fully. And let the worship leading be free from too many words of direction: do nothing to constrain the flow of the Spirit. Its easy to lose yourself for an hour or more in such circumstances.

3. Be real. He's the One with whom I can be transparent, let it all hang out. He is totally trustworthy, knows everything about me and yet never condemns, always loves me. Therefore, there are no barriers. I can be real, let out my anger or frustration, shout, cry, rejoice and revel in his presence.

On the other hand, it may be that the first thing you discover as you seek his face is that he isn't the desire of your heart. To be sure, he has his place in your life, and you may even work full-time for him in his kingdom, but now you realise that somewhere down the track your focus has shifted. It's more on the work and on your ministry than on him. You now realise that you have never sought him for himself and for no other reason than to revel in the intimacy of your relationship. If that is so, be encouraged: if you will submit to his heart surgery, you'll come out with a new lease of life.

Other disturbing thoughts may surface. As you begin to face up to the unexpected shallowness of your heart attitude to Jesus, you may realise that this applies also to your marriage, friendships and other relationships. Indeed, scripture guarantees that there is a connection between them.

It is important not to rush this phase of our approach to God. As we seek his face there will probably be things we need to confess, as well as unresolved issues, to say nothing of incidents from the past which are liable to surface unbidden. Therefore, leave plenty of time to be alone with God - an hour perhaps, a day if possible. This is not a time of introspection, of pulling skeletons from the cupboard, or scraping the bottom of the barrel for another sin to confess. The whole focus in seeking God's face must be on him. In this phase of the process **you ask God to show you what needs to be dealt with**, and you may get some surprises.

As you do this, maintain a flow of worship in your heart. Remind yourself who he is and how he responds to his people (the teaching of Chapters 5 & 6). He is not standing over you with a big stick and a frown on his face. He's not an angry Father. The picture is that of Jesus calling little children to his knee. He doesn't avoid issues or mince words, but he's gentle and gracious with it. You can be open with God as with no other person. With him you can think the unthinkable, pour out your heart in safety, and find peace for your soul.

Depending upon those present, it may be necessary to lead some to Christ, and to get others filled with the Spirit. In leading this phase it may be appropriate also to pronounce absolution and to bless the people. It is a spiritual principle that having dealt with the negative, it must be followed by the positive. After confession and repentance must come absolution and blessing. Then joy will flow unbidden, because your personal relationship with Jesus has been put right. God is gently and graciously widening your horizons, re-ordering your priorities, making you more Christ-like, and therefore changing you from one degree of glory to a higher one (*2 Corinthians 3:18*). Before long you'll find people saying "You're different. What's happened?"!

4. Healing of memories.
Jesus came to set us free from all that the devil has done in our lives. This includes salvation, healing of every kind, and deliverance. His intention is that we live life to the full in the freedom of the Holy Spirit. The means by which he sets us free is his word of truth. Indeed, he himself is the truth (*John 14:6*), so there is a two-fold aspect to being set free. It happens by hearing his word of truth (scripture), and by our personal relationship with him. Thus:

> *To the Jews who had believed him, Jesus said, "If you hold to my teaching, you are really my disciples. Then you will know the truth, and the truth will set you free."*
> *... So if the Son sets you free, you will be free indeed.*
> *(John 8:31,36)*

As with his teaching on worship, Jesus' prescription for inner healing is simple and direct. Sadly, much of what passes for Christian counselling today is a distortion that is liable to leave people in bondage. The crucial truth is that when Christ died on the cross you personally were included, your *old man* died with him. Thus, your past, complete with all its pains, hurts, and traumas is dead and therefore its hold on you *has been broken*.

> *Don't you know that all of us who were baptised into
> Christ Jesus were baptised into his death? We were therefore
> buried with him through baptism into death in order that,
> just as Christ was raised from the dead through the glory
> of the Father, we too may live a new life. (Romans 6:3-4)*

This is not to deny the reality of what happened to you, but to say that, if only you knew it, you have in fact been set free. *By his wounds you **have been** healed (1Peter 2:24).* Once you know this, believe it, and live in the good of it, you are free. It's that simple! The very simplicity of it offends those who love to counsel. Church, we're not meant to wallow in the mud of the past and spend weeks or months in counselling sessions. Christ has set you free so that you can serve and be fruitful in his kingdom. Therefore, get your eyes on him, and do the work of the kingdom in the freedom of the Spirit.

The issue is not what has happened to you, but what you do with it. Results seem to depend upon personality. Some who have suffered terrible abuse break free once they hear and believe the word of truth, and go off like rockets in the kingdom. Others whose hurts are trivial in comparison may remain hostage to them, or at best, limp through life. It's a choice.

One of the main reasons for not entering into your healing is unforgiveness. Unless you forgive others, God cannot forgive you. Some have been so badly hurt that they cannot forgive. Ask them: "Are you willing to let God make you willing to forgive?" Complete healing often follows.

5. Direct counselling [1].

In healing memories, the process is similar to a visit to your medical practitioner. (1) *Diagnosis* of the root cause(s) of the problem. This is done through the 'hearing' gifts of the Spirit. (2) *Prescription and treatment.* Again, the Spirit will give scriptures appropriate to the individual and his/her situation. With severely damaged people this may well be an extended process, with the Spirit revealing deeper issues as and when the person is able to cope. It may also require bringing that person to live for a while in a faith-filled, supportive environment, until they can stand on their own. Note, however, that although the Spirit may pinpoint issues from the past during the diagnosis phase, it is *not* right to take the person back into their past, to rummage about and stir up all the dead and rotting junk now nailed to Christ's cross.

6. Meeting with God.

Up to this point the emphasis has been upon getting ourselves right with God, allowing him to identify and cleanse problem areas. It is always good to intersperse such times with suitable drink and meal breaks, but to maintain a flow of worship throughout. Now, however, having passed the bronze altar and the washing bowl, with cleansed hearts we are ready to give our undivided attention to meeting with God.

Those who have never done this before may be apprehensive, or feel (wrongly, of course), that they will never make it there, even if everyone else does. As always, deal with misconceptions by the application of scripture. Thus:

We know that Christ, risen and exalted, is at the Father's right hand in glory, interceding for us within the very throne room of heaven. Beloved, you are 'in Christ' and if Christ is in the throne room, how can you be anywhere else?! This truth was opened to John on the island of Patmos as he was in the Spirit on the Lord's day.

> *I looked, and there before me was a door standing*
> *open in heaven. And the voice I had first heard*
> *speaking to me like a trumpet said, "Come up here,*
> *and I will show you what must take place after this."*
> *At once I was in the Spirit, and there before me was a*
> *throne in heaven with someone sitting on it. (Revelation 4, 1).*

The activities known as 'seeking the Lord', 'meeting with God', 'entering the Most Holy Place', 'going through the open door in heaven', are all expressions of the same thing. And what do they amount to? Just as the complex symbolism of the tabernacle collapsed into the revelation of God in Christ reconciling the world to himself, so these terms in turn, reduce to the revelation that those who are 'in Christ' belong in the heavenly throne room. This is God's truth about you, if indeed you belong to Christ.

John found that he didn't need to do anything himself to enter God's throne room. It happened at once. The truth is that the only part we play is in desiring to be there. The Spirit does the rest, because that's his job - to reveal Jesus (*John 16:12-15*). Spiritually speaking, you are in the throne room because you are 'in Christ'. Going through the open door' is simply bringing your consciousness into line with that truth.

How do I know?
How do I know that I'm in the Most Holy Place? By faith! God doesn't play tricks on us. When our hearts are set on him he cannot fail to respond (c.f. *Luke 11:11-13*). You are not looking for an experience, you are seeking Jesus' face. Ask to see him. You may not see a picture or vision, but in some way God will impact your spirit, and you will know it.

Don't be phased out if he doesn't respond as soon as you prepare to meet with him. Others may seem to be making it in there ahead of you, but don't let that trouble you. The proof of it is not in what noises people make, or in what they claim to have experienced. Look for the fruit. How has meeting with Jesus changed them and their lifestyle?

The timing and the manner of his meeting with you are for him to determine. If he chooses to treat you as he did the child Samuel, waking you to his presence in the quiet of the night, rather than there in the meeting with the others, so be it. And be open to his touching you in ways you don't expect and haven't experienced before.

There's great variety in meeting with him. He may impact you with a revelation of his love, or his holiness. You may see something of the compassion or grace of Jesus which will blow your socks off. Or it may be he will give you a revelation of his indescribable gentleness. Sometimes there will be very little in the way of feelings, but you will probably have a sense of being in an almost tangible presence, and of deep peace. It's then he's training you to fellowship with him by faith rather than feelings. Whatever the immediate outcome, don't give up. Make seeking his face a permanent part of your daily life.

The voice of God.

Meeting with God is a two-way process, but it's intelligent to leave most of the speaking to him. As King Solomon wrote: *"Do not be quick with your mouth, do not be hasty in your heart to utter anything before God. God is in heaven and you are on earth, so let your words be few." (Ecclesiastes 5:2)*. There is nothing more wonderful on earth than to know that you have heard God. In the Most Holy Place you will adore him, pour out your very being in worship, receive his love, but it is also the place of hearing. One of the reasons for deliberately seeking God's face is to obtain guidance and discern his will (Chapter 4). This generally takes time - see the scriptures in Chapter 9.

It is now that we see why the way into God's presence, first shown to Moses in the form of the tabernacle, is what it is. It is a process of getting in touch with our heart. The more fully we are in touch with our heart, the clearer the voice of God is to us. The pressures of modern life have turned us from human beings into human doings. Therefore it takes time to tune into God's heart, unless you have already established a lifestyle of living in his presence.

His intention is that we shall learn to live in tune with our hearts, wherein he has placed desires that can be satisfied fully only by being in love with him. The point, of course, is that seeking God is no formal path, but the expression of a love affair. And if it is not yet that, it will become so as you seek him with all your heart.

1. We love the place, O God
   Wherein Thine honour dwells
   The joy of Thine abode
   All earthly joy excels.

2. It is the house of prayer
   Wherein Thy servants meet
   And Thou, O Lord, art there
   Thy chosen flock to greet.

3. We love the word of life
   The word that tells of peace
   Of comforts in the strife
   And joys that never cease.

4. We love to sing below
   Of mercies freely given
   But O we long to know
   The triumph song of heaven.

5. Lord Jesus, give us grace
   On earth to love Thee more
   In heaven to see Thy face
   And with Thy saints adore.

William Bullock, 1798-1874

Chapter 11
Living In The Glory

The Jerusalem temple.

In the reign of King Solomon, the tabernacle of King David was replaced by a permanent temple in Jerusalem. In some respects its design was a development of that of the tabernacle of Moses. King David gave Solomon *the plans of all that the Spirit had put in his mind for the courts of the temple of the Lord ....* (1 Chronicles 28:11-12). Specifically of note for our purposes, the Most Holy Place was cubic in shape (*1 Kings 6:19-20*).

The significance of this curious fact is revealed in Revelation 21 where it transpires that the Holy City, the new Jerusalem, is also cubic. The inference is that this is not so much a city such as we are accustomed to, but the very inner sanctuary of heaven itself. Thus, the declaration in a loud voice from the throne saying, *"Now the dwelling of God is with men, and he will live with them. They will be his people, and God himself will be with them and be their God. (Revelation 21:3)* The wheel has come full circle. Once more God and man are living in permanent face-to-face communion on earth, only now 'the fall' is history and there is all eternity to look forward to. That is still to come in all its fullness. Nevertheless, in this life we may live the life of the Most Holy Place.

With God in the Most Holy Place.

What is the difference between life in this place with God, and that in the Holy Place? Just this: in the Holy Place there is fellowship with each other, there is the ministry of the word, and ministry to each other through the gifts of the Spirit. In the Most Holy Place it is God and you, one to one. Total reality. Stillness. Peace. Everything is transparent. The awesomeness of God is overshadowing. Emphasis shifts from the gifts of the Spirit to the fruit of the Spirit.

Life in the Holy Place, charismatic style, could be lived part-time and it didn't show too much. This is not true of the Most Holy Place. God now becomes all-consuming: you want to be with Him all the time, the thirst and hunger after His presence becomes a constant in your life. You begin to live to pray. Go short on prayer for a single day and those who are moving to the same drumbeat notice the difference in you, and you yourself are painfully and immediately aware of a lack of power for service and ministry. It's serious business. You can't go back to the old ways; you can't even mark time. As never before you find that the life you now live is not your life, but the life which Christ lives in you. You are His bondservant. A stricter holiness is required.

Solomon's throne.

To fellowship with God within the veil is not a static experience repeated indefinitely. Our many-splendoured God touches us in an infinite variety of ways, thereby ensuring the freshness of our relationship with him. Fellowshipping with God within the veil is but a way of talking of our new life in Christ. In it there should be a progression of increasing maturity and intimacy. This is clearly prefigured by the account of Solomon's throne, which was approached by six steps and a footstool.

> *Then the king made a great throne inlaid with ivory and overlaid with pure gold. The throne had six steps, and a footstool of gold was attached to it. On both sides of the seat were armrests, with a lion standing beside each of them. Twelve lions stood on the six steps, one at either end of each step. Nothing like it had ever been made for any other kingdom. (2 Chronicles 9:17-19)*

This throne is a model of our approach to Christ enthroned in glory. It speaks to us of increasing intimacy and awesomeness as draw closer to the throne of our God, and of a developing lifestyle. Enoch walked this path and became so absorbed in his life with God, and pleased God so much (*Hebrews 11:5*), that he didn't die: there was a smooth and effortless transition to heaven, for God simply took him away and *he was no more (Genesis 5:24)*.

Queen Esther: Intimacy with God.

The Tabernacle speaks to us of a progress into God's presence. Solomon's throne holds out the possibility of increasing depths of fellowship with God within the throne room. A yet more amazing prospect is suggested by the story of Queen Esther.

Esther is a type of the church, and King Artaxerxes represents God. Before Esther is permitted to enter the King's presence she must submit to a lengthy period of preparation during which evidence of the old way of life is first removed and then replaced with the sweet fragrance of Christ-likeness. The key issue is this: when she enters the King's presence it is solely and entirely to give *him* the greatest possible pleasure. She is there to delight and captivate him, without thought of self. Whatever he desires, she will respond accordingly. Total abandonment to his will is the King's desire for us.

There is, therefore, a progressive revelation in the history of the OT in respect of the intimacy God wants with those in his kingdom. First comes the Holy of Holies revelation. Then, roughly 250 years later, Solomon's throne. Finally, Esther, dated from late in the post-exilic period and therefore one of the last books of the OT canon to be written, with its tantalising slant on intimacy of the deepest kind, written in story language that sticks in the memory. It was God's last word on the subject, until Jesus came.

The lifestyle of the Most Holy Place.

To seek God's face and his righteousness, to meet with him in the Most Holy Place and remain in his rest, is meant to be the foundation of our lifestyle. We begin with times when we step aside specifically to fellowship with him for greater or lesser periods. As this is established in our economy, the influence of these encounters gradually extends beyond the time spent consciously in his presence, until they run into each other and thus become our lifestyle.

We discover that we are living on two levels simultaneously, the natural and the supernatural. We are dealing at any given moment with whatever circumstances demand, but at the same time we are seeing and hearing in the Spirit. Thereby, all life, even the mundane and routine, is consecrated.

Scripture is rich in synonyms of the life of heaven lived on earth, the life that we enter by faith and maintain by keeping our eyes fixed on Jesus. Thus, we walk in the light, live by the Spirit, enter the promised land, fellowship with God in the Most Holy Place, minister as priests after the order of Melchisedek, and become Christ-like. All these amount to the same thing: a lifestyle of intimate fellowship with God. For this we were created and have our being. One of the most helpful of these synonyms is that of entering God's rest.

God's rest.

God promises his people 'rest' as the final state of the elect, when strife with evil will have ceased, and the full harvest been brought in of all the good works prepared for his people since before the foundation of the world.

> *Then I heard a voice from heaven say, "Write: Blessed are the dead who die in the Lord from now on."*

> *"Yes," says the Spirit, "they will rest from their labour,*
> *for their deeds will follow them." (Revelation 14:13)*

This is yet to come. Jesus, however, promised his followers rest for your souls in this earthly life.

> *"Come to me, all you who are weary and burdened,*
> *and I will give you rest. Take my yoke upon you*
> *and learn from me, for I am gentle and humble in heart,*
> *and you will find rest for your souls. For my yoke is*
> *easy and my burden is light." (Matthew 11:28-30)*

The condition of entering this 'rest' is to take my yoke upon you and learn from me. To 'rest' in this sense in not to stop working but to live and act under the Father's direction, as did Jesus. Humility (literally, lowliness of mind) is the key because it is an attitude of submission to the Father's will. The 'yoke' is still there because there is work to be done, but he provides the direction and shoulders the load with us so that the *burden is light*. There is no striving in it because *it is God who works in you to will and to act according to his good purpose (Philippians 2:13)*.

To the Jews of Jesus' day the 'rest' offered in doing the will of God was in stark contrast to the draining effort required in their futile attempts to keep the law of Moses by self-effort and regulation. Specifically, he gives *rest for your souls*. To enter God's rest is to be at peace in what we are doing, which may be extremely demanding, because we know that we are doing his will. It is a lifestyle free from striving, tension and stress because our minds are set upon his purpose for our lives.

This 'rest' is entered by faith. Faith is the action we take in obedience to God's word of direction. In *Hebrews* we find that the Israelis under Moses failed to enter God's 'rest' because of unbelief (which is the absence of faith). They refused to enter the promised land when God told them to. Many Christians, similarly, refuse to go beyond the basic step of salvation. But God's desire is that we all enter into the life of the Most Holy Place and live in such continual communion with him then we are truly at rest in our souls and fruitful in our lives. Thus, this 'rest' is but a manner of speaking about the life of the Most Holy Place in which we share in God's own rest which he himself entered on completing his work of creation (*Genesis 2:2*). Indeed, according to Genesis, man's first day on earth was one of rest.

Jesus said that we should take his yoke and learn of him. Learning is a process. Entering God's rest is about developing a life of intimate fellowship with him, learning to let him do all for us and in us. It is to cease from initiative and self-effort, and to yield in full surrender of faith to his desires.

> *Anyone who enters God's rest also rests from his own work, just as God did from his (Hebrews 4:10).*

The exhortation to *make every effort to enter that rest (Hebrews 4:11)* is not in conflict with the above teaching. It refers simply to a continuing act of will, that of keeping our focus on seeking God's face, and of obedience to him. Therefore *Let us fix our eyes on Jesus, the author and perfector of our faith (Hebrews 12:2)*.

1. Lord, I believe a rest remains
   To all Thy people known
   A rest where pure enjoyment reigns
   And Thou art loved alone.

2. A rest, where all our soul's desire
   Is fixed on things above
   Where fear and sin and grief expire
   Cast out by perfect love.

3. O that I now the rest might know
   Believe and enter in!
   Now, Saviour, now the power bestow
   And let me cease from sin.

4. Remove this hardness from my heart
   This unbelief remove
   To me the rest of faith impart
   The sabbath of Thy love.

> 5 I would be Thine, Thou know'st I would
>   And have Thee all my own
>   Thee, O my all-sufficient Good
>   I want, and Thee alone.
>
> 6. Thy name to me, Thy nature grant
>   This, only this be given
>   Nothing beside my God I want
>   Nothing in earth or heaven.

Charles Wesley (1707-88)

Ministry to man

As priests we are to minister to both God and man, especially in the context of evangelism. Thus Paul described himself as *"a minister of Christ Jesus to the Gentiles with the priestly duty of proclaiming the gospel of God" (Romans 15:16)*. However, our priestly ministry in the church and the world comes out of our ministry to God in the Most Holy Place.

> *They [the Macedonians] gave themselves first to the Lord and then to us in keeping with God's will. (2 Corinthians 8:5)*

The principle is found in *Ezekiel 44*. Those who are wholeheartedly loyal to God, whose greatest joy is to seek his face without ulterior motives, are the ones he can trust with power-filled ministry to men. They will seek no position or glory for themselves. They are content that he himself is their portion and their exceedingly great reward. This is the test by which true ministry shall be recognised. Christ himself will honour them before our Father in heaven.

> *So you also, when you have done everything you were told to do, should say, 'We are unworthy servants; we have only done our duty.'" (Luke 17:10)*

The Lord said to Aaron, ... "I am your share and your inheritance among the Israelites". (Numbers 18:20)

"I am to be the only inheritance the priests have. ... I will be their possession (Ezekiel 44:28)

> 1. Eternal Light! Eternal Light!
> How pure the soul must be,
> When placed within Thy searching sight,
> It shrinks not, but, with calm delight,
> Can live, and look on Thee!
>
> 2. There is a way for man to rise
> To that sublime abode:
> An offering and a sacrifice,
> A Holy Spirit's energies,
> An Advocate with God.
>
> 3. These, these prepare us for the sight
> Of holiness above,
> The sons of ignorance and night
> May dwell in the eternal Light
> Through the eternal Love.
>
> Thomas Binney (1798-1874)

"Now devote your heart and soul to seeking the LORD your God. Begin to build the sanctuary of the LORD God, so that you may bring the ark of the covenant of the LORD and the sacred articles belonging to God into the temple that will be built for the Name of the LORD." (1 Chronicles 22:19)

REFERENCES

Chapter 1
1.1 *Another Wave of Revival* Frank Bartelman, Whitaker House, 1982, USA.

Chapter 3
3.1 E.C. Blackman, p145 in *A Theological Word Book of the Bible* A. Richardson (Ed), SCM Press, London 1950.

3.2 *The Art of Prayer* Compiled by Igumen Chariton, Trans. by E. Kadloubovsky & E.M. Palmer, Faber & Faber, London 1966.

Chapter 5
5.1 *The Distinctive Ideas of the Old Testament* N.H. Snaith, Epworth Press, London 1944.

Chapter 6
6.1 Ref. 5.1.
6.2 *From Mercy to Majesty* Colin Urquhart, Hodder & Stoughton, London 1995, p69.
6.3 *Expository Dictionary of Bible Words* W.E. Vine, Marshall Morgan & Scott, Basingstoke, Hants., England, 1981.
6.4 Colin Urquhart, Pastoral Letter, March 1999.

Chapter 7
7.1 D.M. Adams, personal translation.

Chapter 10
10.1 *The Truth That Sets You Free* Colin Urquhart, Hodder & Stoughton, London 1993, is required reading on this subject.

SCRIPTURE INDEX

Genesis	
1:26	17
2:2	123
2:3	59
2:8	17
2:18	106
5:24	120
12:3	71
14:18	32
25:22	50
39:4	68
49:8-10	32
Exodus	
3:5	59
6:7	20
12:16	63
16:19-20	92
16:23	62
19:6	62
24:11	79
25-31	23
31:13	63
Leviticus	
6:8-13	86,92
16:2,12-13	77
19:18	107
20:26	59
21	32
27:22-24,28	62
Numbers	
6:2	61
18:20	125
23:19	71
Deuteronomy	
4:29	40,47
6:4-5	107
6:10-15	20
6:25	33
7:6-11	20

28	54
Joshua	
6:18-21	60,61
7:13	61
Judges	
18:5	50
1Samuel	
10:8	101
23:4	50
30:8	50
2Samuel	
2:1	50
5:19	50
21:1	51
1Kings	
6:19-20	118
22:5,7	48
2Kings	
13:4	49
1Chronicles	
6:31-32	86
10:13-14	54
16:10	51
16:11	52
22:19	125
28:9	47
28:11-12	118
2Chronicles	
7:14	53
9:17-19	120
14:7	53
15:2,4,12	49,50
15:15	53
18:4	48
20:3	48
20:4	49
20:18-21	86
24:18	54
26:5	53

31:21	54	89:34	72
33:12-13	49	91:4	72
34:3	102	91:14	67
Ezra		96:9	64
6:21	102	97:2	102
Psalms		101:6	86
5:3	99	103:13	67
14:2	45	105:3	51
18:25-26	58	105:4	52
22:26	51	119:2	40,52
26:8	23	119:10	48
27:4	41	119:45	52
27:8	41	119:58	38
27:14	99	119:90	71
30:5	108	119:105	53,88
33:20	99	123:2	102
34:4,10	52	130:5-6	99
36:5	71	139:23-24	47
37:7,34	99	**Proverbs**	
38:15	99	3:34	68
40:1	99	8:17	40,45
40:16	51	28:5	103
46:4	93	**Ecclesiastes**	
46:10	99	5:2	115
51:17	47	**Song of Songs**	
53:2	45	2:4	66
55:9	40	3:2	41
59:9	99	7:10-12	40
63:1	41	**Isaiah**	
69:32	51	8:19	51
70:4	51	26:8	99
73:2-3,13,16-17	101	26:9	41
77:2	49	30:18	99
78:4	42	38:17	67
81:10	94	40:25	61
83:16	49	45:15	16
84:1-2	41	49:15	67
85:10	72	50:1	20
89:14	102	51:1	103

53:12	79	**Hosea**	
55:6-7	109	4:6	54
55:8-9	40,101	5:15	46
57:15	60	6:3	38,109
64:4	100	10:12	103
64:7	38	11:4	66
65:10	52	11:8-9	61,70
66:2	47	12:6	100
Jeremiah		14:2	107
1:12	72	**Joel**	
3:6-10	20	2:12	48
7:23	20	**Amos**	
11:4	20	5:4	52
13:24-25	54,55	**Jonah**	
17:5,9-10	47	2:2	49
21:2	51	3:8	48
23:18,22	50	**Micah**	
26:19	54	7:7	100
29:13	40,48	**Habakkuk**	
31:3	66	2:1,3	101
31:33	21	**Zephaniah**	
33:11	95	1:4,6	55
33:19-26	72	2:3	103
42:7	101	3:8	100
50:4	46	**Zechariah**	
Lamentations		8:22	49
3:22-23	67,71	12:10	68
3:24,26	100	**Malachi**	
Ezekiel		3:18	63
16:8	20	**Matthew**	
20:1	51	6:33	38,46,103
22:26	62	7:7	48
36:26	21	11:27	78
36:28	20	11:28-30	122
44:1ff	124	**Mark**	
44:28	125	12:28-31	107
Daniel		12:30	21
9:13	55	14:38	100

Luke
4:5-8	87
9:23	86
11:9-10	38
11:11-13	114
17:10	124
22:31-32	81

John
3:16	67
4:23-24	87
6:1ff	79
6:35	25
7:29	25
7:39	41
8:1ff	82
8:12	25
8:23	25
8:31,36	111
8:48	93
10:4	93
10:16	74
12:24-25	86
14:6	25,37,78,111
14:9-11	25,78
16:12-15	114
17:14	64
19:34	25
20:23	89

Acts
1:4	100
3:25	109
6:7	77
13:38-39	26
17:26-28	42,50

Romans
1:17	33,104
2:4	70
3:21-24	33
6:3-4	112
6:19	82
8:26-27	80
8:31	81
8:33-34	80,83
10:12	52
11:11	74
12:1	63,95
12:11	38
13:8	33
15:16	124

1Corinthians
1:2	64
1:9	71
5:7	33
6:19	64
10:13	81
14:32	109
15:31	86

2Corinthians
1:12	62
3:18	111
4:4	78
5:17	104
8:5	124
13:4	82

Galatians
3:26-27	104
3:28	104
4:4-7	104
5:24	87

Ephesians
1:3-4	22,63
2:11-3:6	74,76
2:12	18
2:14-19	74,75
3:12	25,83

Philippians
1:6	81
2:13	122

Colossians	
1:15	78
3:17	78
1Thessalonians	
4:3-4,7	64
1Timothy	
1:16	69
2:4	70
2:5	78
2Timothy	
1:7	109
2:13	71
Titus	
2:12	96
Hebrews	
1:3	78
2:11	64
2:17	27
4:5	101
4:10	123
4:11	123
4:15-16	27,83,105
5:1	78
5:13	102
7:1-3	32
7:12	33
7:16	78
7:17-19	33
7:25	81
9:4	76,90
10:20	25
10:19-22	25,63,102
10:20	24,34
10:29	43
11:5	120
11:6	38,46,48
12:2	82,123
12:10	64
12:14	64

13:15	95
1Peter	
1:15-16	64
2:9	26
2:24	112
2Peter	
1:4	21
1John	
2:1-2	80
3:17	68
4:7-21	107
4:16	65
4:19	52,65
Revelation	
3:15-16	46
4:1-2	46,113
5:6	79
14:13	122
21:2-3	19,118,119

Further copies of this title and copies of
the other two books by David M. Adams
can be purchased on-line from

www.theway.co.uk

or by contacting

Harvest Fields Distribution
Unit 17 Churchill Business Park
Churchill Road
DONCASTER
DN1 2TF
UK

Tel: +44 (0)1302 367868
Fax: +44 (0)1302 361006